PROFITABLE
CONSULTING

ROBERT O. METZGER, Ph.D., CMC

ADDISON-WESLEY PUBLISHING COMPANY, INC.
Reading, Massachusetts   Menlo Park, California   New York
Don Mills, Ontario   Wokingham, England   Amsterdam
Bonn   Sydney   Singapore   Tokyo   Madrid   San Juan

PROFITABLE
CONSULTING

·

GUIDING
AMERICA'S
MANAGERS
INTO THE
NEXT
CENTURY

·

Library of Congress Cataloging-in-Publication Data

Metzger, Robert O.
  Profitable consulting : helping American managers face the future
/ Robert O. Metzger.
      p.   cm.
  Bibliography: p.
  Includes index.
  ISBN 0-201-09539-4
  1. Business consultants—United States.   2. Industrial management—
United States.   I. Title.   HD69.C6M47   1988   658.4'6—dc19
88-15476

Copyright © 1989 by Addison-Wesley Publishing Company, Inc.

Sponsoring editor, Scott Shershow
Production coordinator, Lynne Reed
Cover design by Marge Anderson
Text design by Janis Capone
Set in 11 point Bodoni Book by Compset Inc., Beverly, MA

ISBN 0-201-09539-4
ABCDEFGHIJ-DO-898
First printing, October 1988

To Joelle
My daughter and my best friend

CONTENTS

PREFACE   xi

CHAPTER 1   **INTERESTING TIMES** ▪ 2
  5 Organization Life Cycles
  7 Self-Denial
  9 Genetic Imprinting
  13 Global Concepts
  14 Global Competition
  15 Global Compensation
  16 Ready, Fire, Aim!
  16 Cost Management—A New Driving Force
  17 Bigger Is Not Always Better
  18 Deregulation—A Barrel of Fun
  19 Fiber Optics, Anyone?
  19 A Teddy Bear with Every Car Loan
  21 Hard Issues and Easy Solutions
  23 Recommended Readings

CHAPTER 2   **AN INDUSTRY COMES OF AGE** ▪ 24
  25 Growth and Expansion
  28 From Manager to Consultant
  29 Specialties and Specialists
  31 Global Consulting
  33 Consolidation of Large Consulting Firms
  35 The Academic Independent
  38 Consolidation of Industry Organizations
  41 Decline and Fall
  42 Recommended Readings

CHAPTER 3   **NEW STANDARDS** ▪ 44
  46 More Demanding Clients
  47 What You Know and Who You Know

49 A Shift from Content to Process . . .
50 . . . And Back Again
52 Content Consulting Lives—In City Hall
53 New Methodologies
55 Training the Trainer
55 New Consultants for New Clients
58 Recommended Readings

CHAPTER 4   **THE NEW MARKETING** ▪ 60
61 Tougher Clients, Tougher Sales
62 Getting Quoted
63 Getting Published
65 Taking Off the Gloves
69 Getting a Computer
70 The State of the Art
72 Recommended Readings

CHAPTER 5   **NEW STRATEGIC SERVICES** ▪ 74
75 Old Models, New Paradigms
77 Action and Reaction
78 The Exponential Curve of Change
81 Becoming the 800-Pound Gorilla
83 Developing Competitive Advantage
85 Client Strategic Needs
88 Managing Strategic Planning Retreats
90 Back to the Basics
91 The Red Queen Syndrome and the Inevitability
of Change
93 Recommended Readings

CHAPTER 6   **NEW ORGANIZATION DESIGNS** ▪ 94
95 The Good Old Days
96 Past and Future
98 Work Design
103 Principles of Self-Design

105 Installing a Self-Design Program
108 The Schmenner Slope
110 Recommended Readings

CHAPTER 7 **NEW CHALLENGES IN COMPENSATION ▪ 112**
113 Reward Systems of the Machine Bureaucracy
116 Pay for Performance
118 Profit and Gain Sharing
119 Determining Standards of Performance
122 Improving Performance and Coping with Change
124 Compensation and Corporate Renewal
125 Learning the Ropes
126 Recommended Readings

CHAPTER 8 **NEW MARKETING SERVICES ▪ 128**
129 Outmoded Thinking
131 American Products and Foreign Tastes
135 Joint Ventures and Creative Distribution
138 Olivetti—A New Role Model
140 Macro- and Micro-level Assistance
142 Going Back to School
143 Recommended Readings

CHAPTER 9 **NEW TECHNOLOGIES, OPERATIONS AND SYSTEMS SUPPORT ▪ 144**
145 Defining the Problem
146 Management Issues
147 Manufacturing Issues
149 The Need for Specific Objectives
149 Simplistic Approaches to Complex Problems
152 "Balloon-Breaking" and the "Bonzo-Banana" Culture
154 How Much Automation, Anyway?
155 Technology Training—The Next Great Market

CONTENTS

157   Artificial Intelligence—The Real 2001 System
159   Exciting Possibilities
160   Recommended Readings

CHAPTER 10   **TODAY'S LESSONS AND TOMORROW'S CONSULTANTS ▪ 162**

163   Helping the Human Process
164   Consulting to Small Businesses
167   Consulting to Family Businesses
172   Everything Has a Five-Year Obsolescence—Including Us
173   Administrative Space Stations
175   Preventing Classic Errors
178   Automation Means Fewer Experts
179   Up and Running
180   Who Gets The Deceased's Royalties?
181   Implications of Public Ownership
183   Client Power
184   Recommended Readings

INDEX   **187**

x

PREFACE

It has been an eventful seven years since I first sat down to write a book entitled *Consulting to Management*. That book was developed primarily to help solve a specific problem: the dearth of teaching materials on the subject of management consulting skills for our M.B.A. students at the University of Southern California. Never did Larry Greiner, my co-author, or I envision the book's becoming the "standard" in most graduate consulting skills programs, and certainly not on a worldwide basis. However, sales of the book have been tremendous in Singapore, Australia, Britain and throughout Europe, and Canada. A number of lions of the industry gave us very complimentary reviews, and Jim Kennedy of *Consultants News* even listed it as *the* basic book neophytes should own. The Institute of Management Consultants helped promote the book through a very aggressive membership program, and ACME has featured the book on its "Suggested Reading" list for the past four years. All told, *Consulting to Management* established several mail-order sales records for the publisher.

But where *Consulting to Management* addresses basic consulting skills and issues, *Profitable Consulting* focuses on the more sophisticated aspects of the profession. It picks up where the first book left off, discussing contemporary issues in strategic planning, marketing, organization, compensation, work design, and automation in more detail. Most important, it evaluates and explores the changes in the industry that have come about since 1982. And there certainly have been many. In the Preface to *Consulting to Management*, we wrote about the on-going need for management consultants to assist clients in dealing with the then recent deregulation of the airline, financial services, and telecommunications industries; the embryonic growth of totally new industries such as home computers and biotechnology; and the titanic struggle by Detroit's big-3 automotive manufacturers to survive the Japanese onslaught in the early 1980s. Since then, we have seen continued upheaval, competition, takeovers, and failures in the airline and banking industries; a settling out of the new competition in telecommunications; the renaissance of Ford and Chrysler; GE's sale of its consumer products division to the French, its redeployment of its blue-collar work force, which reduced unionized labor by 50 percent; CBS's sale of its record division to the Japanese; the obsolescence of vinyl records by digital discs and now digital tapes; new vaccines and herbicides from biotechnology; a host of new pharmaceutical products; the rise and impact of robotics; the Japanese now threatened by the Koreans and Chinese; OPEC in some state of disarray; GM's failure to create the hoped-for synergy needed between its automotive, aerospace, and information systems organizations; and the surfacing of many critical issues that continue to threaten our client organizations and their strategies.

Of equal or greater impact have been the continued pressure on American managers to take early retirement; increased automation reducing both blue-collar and skilled ranks; the shift from *Fortune* 1,000 employment to employment by firms of under 100 people; and the explosion of entrepreneurship programs at major business schools across the country. Simultaneously, new systems, adopting satellite communications channels to transmit administrative data from offshore clerical centers with very inexpensive labor, have begun undermining clerical jobs and entry-level opportunities in the work force. Further, in just the past five years, major multinationals have aggressively expanded their international alliances to better compete in global markets while reducing the volume and size of their consulting contracts.

Those consulting firms that continue to be in constant demand are finding more experienced and smarter clients who have no time for lengthy, detailed written reports and who prefer "process" consultants who facilitate needed change rather than "content" consultants who teach basic management techniques or methodologies by example.

Perhaps no less critical from my own perspective is the settling out that has taken place in the consulting industry. Major firms such as Cresap, McCormick and Paget, Temple, Barker & Sloane, Nolan-Norton, Kaplan-Smith and Hay & Associates all have been acquired by even larger firms, some of them from overseas, and even Arthur D. Little was threatened briefly by a hostile takeover not long ago. Other major firms such as MAC and Booz, Allen have significantly restructured their U.S.-based operations, while McKinsey & Co. actually began recruiting graduates from other than Harvard, Wharton, or Stanford. The biggest firms have begun to develop their own international, if not global, alliances with foreign professional firms, while more and more foreign consultants find bridgeheads in U.S. markets.

Collectively these changes have created a totally new paradigm within which consultants must work if they are to be successful into the next century. The pressure on consulting firms, on their managing partners, and especially on independents is tremendous: to return to school, to develop contacts with academics and state-of-the-art researchers, to develop international friendships and global alliances, and to specialize as never before. This book attempts to address this whirlwind of client and consultant change in the perspective of what will be required from individual professionals and consulting firms alike through the 1990s and past the year 2000. It is about the new demands on consultants and the new consultants themselves.

In describing and discussing these issues, two major themes emerge. The first is that clients want and need more process services than they have in the past, yet demand that such non-specific support be delivered by consultants who are very specific in their industry knowledge. The second is that the consulting industry is more successful than ever at a time when many of its original organizations and concepts are disappearing. These two themes surface again and again, and they are very telling in what they imply.

Many of the consulting approaches and techniques explored in this book—such as organizational self-design, Schmenner's services slope, or corporate decline and death—are extremely complex. Consultants already using these concepts and models directly or in modified form will appreciate that their applications differ from industry to industry and organization to organization. Therefore, although this book covers a wider range of subject matter than *Consulting to Management*, it does so strategically and philosophically, relying on far less detail. Gone are the sample forms, letters, and pictograms for tyros. Somewhere about 1985, the mythical firm of **Charles, Cranston, Kato & Kent** was absorbed by a Singaporean conglomerate. And as with any work with such ambitious objectives, whatever knowledge I might share in this book only pales beside my ignorance on these matters.

No such book would ever come into being without the unselfish assistance of many, many people. Principal among my supporters were Warren Bennis, Harry Bernhard, Dick Mason, and Bob Sabath, who gave of their invaluable time to read my manuscripts, adding their thoughts and expertise; the many graduate students at U.S.C. who keep asking the damnedest questions, forcing me to continue my quest for the truth; Scott Shershow, my editor, who has shown the patience of a saint and the business skills of a Hollywood agent; and most of all, Alan Glassman, who helped me coalesce many of my thoughts into clear issues and models. Finally, the book has its roots in the challenges and opportunities articulated by my clients and in their desire to allow me to participate with them in planning for the future. Thank you so much—one and all.

Robert O. Metzger, Ph.D., CMC
Santa Ana, California
June 1988

PROFITABLE
CONSULTING

CHAPTER 1

INTERESTING

TIMES

There is an old Chinese curse: "May you live in interesting times." For better or for worse, these are exactly the sort of times management consultants find themselves living and working in as the twentieth century draws to a close. It is a time filled with conflicts and contradictions, among clients and within the consulting profession itself. This book is about those conflicts and these times, and about an emerging new kind of management consultant—well aware of the old, mechanistic management values of the 1950s, 1960s and early 1970s, but able to apply flexible, creative, organic solutions to client organizations desperate for rebirth and renewal. To better understand what is happening to the consulting industry, we first must attempt to understand what has been happening to our clients.

Over the past decade enormous pressures have come to bear against American industry. If someone were to synthesize all the articles in *Forbes, Business Week, Fortune,* the *Harvard Business Review, Sloan Management Review,* and other leading business publications that have attempted to address the problems and weaknesses of U.S.-based companies, the topics could be broken down along the following lines:

- American industry must match the quality of Asian and European products;
- American industry must attain per unit production costs on a parity with foreign competitors;
- American industry must greatly improve levels of worker productivity; and
- American industry must gain expertise in selling American products in global markets.

Collectively, these reports tell the story of an old, obsolete paradigm of management in the process of being overtaken by a new one that reflects the globalization of business, markets, and competition. Not all these issues affect all American companies in the same way, even now; and, some very well-managed American firms such as Hewlett-Packard, Omark Industries,

3M and General Electric, to name just a few, have always tran-scended many of the limitations of the old paradigm. On the other hand, international markets do dominate many sectors of business today, and to compete successfully in them requires a totally different set of values and completely new organization structures compared to what drove American industry in the past thirty years.

All this is perfectly clear, but it is still difficult to grasp just what *is* troubling American industry. Why is it so inefficient? Specifically, what can consultants do in the next decade to re-verse this apparent national malaise? Many people have at-tempted answers to these questions—Peters and Waterman, Gilbreath, Bennis, O'Toole, Davis, Mintzberg, Brian-Quinn, and Toffler. Each sees a set of multiple issues from his own learned perspective, and each, in his own way, is correct. But how can we bring all this thinking together into one coherent model with which management consultants can understand the problems clients have; develop and implement solutions for them that work; and at the same time, prevent consultants them-selves from becoming obsolete? As the futurist Alvin Toffler asks, "How can we prevent ourselves from providing 'second wave' solutions to 'third wave' problems?"

This book is about these basic questions. There are many who would say that the worst of the turmoil in American manage-ment, and industry in particular, that followed the oil embargoes of the mid-1970s is over and that American managers have learned how to compete effectively. Their proof, simplistically, is the steady growth in the American economy during the eight years of the Reagan administration coupled with the record low levels of unemployment. But the truth is that the United States is now a net debtor nation and that debt is growing; moreover, Americans continue to prefer and demand the quality and pric-ing of foreign goods. Few American firms export and even they have increased their export levels only as faith in the American economy and the value of the U.S. dollar have waned. It has been largely currency speculation, not productivity improvement, that allowed for competitively priced American goods. Furthermore, in industries that were deregulated in the late 1970s and early 1980s—such as airlines, financial services, transportation, and telecommunications—companies are still struggling to find new goals, values, and cultures that will allow them to stay in business.

ORGANIZATION LIFE CYCLES

The problem, I believe, is best conceptualized through the use of a model devised by Christopher Clarke and Simon Pratt of A. T. Kearney in London. It is based on the "organization life cycle" concept. Simply stated, all organizations go through clearly definable stages: *Birth, Growth, Maturity* and *Decline*. And in each stage, they require different types of managers to direct them successfully.

5

The *Birth* stage is a time of entrepreneurship and requires a "Champion" to set the vision and goals of the organization and provide the creative leadership needed to sustain a new idea and a new enterprise. But Champions build organic organizations: steeped in new ideas, oriented toward getting things done in any way possible, driven by emotions and intuition-based decisions. Such organic organizations are unique and marvelous environments to experience. But if the Champion is successful—as Steven Jobs was at Apple or Head was with his ski company—then the enterprise must eventually pass into a *Growth* stage in which it must be led, not by the original Champion but by a "Tank Commander"—someone unafraid to break through enemy territory without regard for the supply lines.

General George Patton, the quintessential "Tank Commander", when once challenged by his superiors about his "precarious" position, replied: "Do you want to send me supplies, or should I give the last 30 miles back?"

The Tank Commander maintains the organic environment with creative marketing, aggressive market penetration, and opportunistic horizontal acquisitions of smaller competitors.

With success, the enterprise has expanded to multiple plants, district sales managers, strategic planners, in-house lawyers, and so forth. This is known as the *Maturity* stage, which is best directed by a "Housekeeper." Organization structures, policy, and procedures rule the day. It is a very mechanistic organization, steeped in formality and built on the basis of control. It is what Henry Mintzberg calls "the machine bureaucracy." Machine bureaucracies have very clear delineations between senior management, operations, and staff. Senior management maintains most of the authority and power in the organization. It makes the policy and formulates the strategic plans. Operations maintains production and implements the strategic plans, while staff attempts to assure as few deviations from policy and standards as possible. This is done through time and motion studies, productivity programs, job training, the creation of specific organization charts filled with narrow job descriptions, performance standards, quality controls, and so forth. Machine bureaucracies have no tolerances for change. All of management's energies go toward keeping the lid on the organization so that production can continue uninterrupted. Managers are rewarded for developing tight operating procedures in such organizations, not for risk taking or testing new ideas. Yet machine bureaucracies seethe with turmoil due to the narrow definitions that permeate everything from job responsibilities to territorial authority. They breed internal conflict and corporate politics that demand senior management keep the lid on ever tighter to control and maximize output.

As markets and entire industries mature, sales flatten, there is little product differentiation, technology is no longer proprietary, and decline sets in. Tom Peters continues the picture of the organization life cycle by arguing that organizations in the Decline stage require what he calls "Lemon Squeezers"—managers who can sell off all the unproductive product lines and subsidiaries, keep the few remaining profitable "cash cows," and use those funds to generate rebirth and renewal again. The environment of the Lemon Squeezer is both mechanistic and organic: mechanistic, in that cost containment programs must be developed, and poor performing assets and businesses are being reevaluated and sold to the highest bidder; and, organic in that new opportunities and markets and Champions are being sought to bring the organization to rebirth and renewal.

This is a usable concept, but Clarke and Pratt take us only so far. Their model still doesn't answer the most important question for consultants: Why do managers and executives allow their businesses to go past the Maturity stage into Decline? Alan Glassman, professor of management at Cal State Northridge, argues that we must add the idea of *Managerial Self-Denial* to understand the business cycle fully.

SELF-DENIAL

The famous Kübler-Ross model of the psychological stages of the terminally ill patient is also a good description of organization decline and death. After learning that they have a fatal malady, patients first seem to enter a period of *Self-Denial* and *Isolation*. They keep to themselves and refuse to accept the diagnosis. This is followed by a period of *Anger*, "Why me?" "It's just not fair!" and so forth. A stage of *Bargaining* follows, "God, just give me one more chance! If you give me just one more year. . . ." *Depression* then sets in, followed finally, by *Acceptance*. If we review the firms we each know that are in decline and approaching organizational failure (death), we can see the same traits projected by management: a refusal to face facts, denial; anger, usually at "unfair" trade barriers and "foreign dumping"; bargaining, usually with a Congressman in the hopes of winning trade tariffs; depression; and finally acceptance. William Hall, in his massive research into eight declining American industries, points out that the external pressures that failing companies in these industries most often complain about are just their final death knells. In almost every case, the current failure can be traced back ten or even twenty years to a poor strategy decision taken when management still had flexibility and time to maneuver.

As consultants, we must help managers in companies in Decline get to the acceptance stage soon enough— so that the Lemon Squeezers can work their "magic" and the company can be "born again" before it really is too late.

We still haven't learned how and why well-educated, intelligent, articulate executives allow themselves to get into the stages of decline and, eventually, corporate death. Chris Argyris may provide an answer in his analysis of what he calls "defensive routines" performed by key individuals in large organizations when facing massive change. According to Argyris, such managers will agree that the rigid, machine bureaucracy is no longer appropriate for their organization, will give enormous resources to create a new and more positive system, but will only end up creating a bigger and better machine bureaucracy! How is it possible? The answer is that this response pattern really is not their fault.

GENETIC IMPRINTING

These senior managers of the 1980s are the product of their 1960s management education and were influenced by mentors who were the product of the 1940s and 1950s. During that period, and on through much of the 1960s, the industries and enterprises begun after World War II were rapidly reaching their maturity stage. Housekeepers, not Champions or Tank Commanders, were required to keep these increasingly large, successful organizations running. They had experienced explosive growth in the 1950s and 1960s and now required mechanistic environments in order to achieve the "maximization of Experience Curves Models" and other management tools of the times. So when their companies entered decline in the 1970s and early 1980s and attempts were made to reverse lagging performance, the best the Housekeepers could do was create a bigger and better machine bureaucracy.

Similar behavior is found in parents who abuse their children. In almost every case, these parents were abused by their parents. They swear that they will never abuse their own kids, and yet when given the opportunity, they repeat the mistakes of their parents, regardless of their education or intelligence levels. Researchers in the field call it "behavioral genetic imprinting." Senior executives in machine bureaucracies have similar behav-

ioral genetic imprinting with respect to managing as Housekeepers, first, last, and always. The problem continues in some
of our oldest and largest industries with no end in sight.

■**CASE IN POINT**
Throughout the 1980s, while Ford and Chrysler, led by Tank
Commanders Petersen and Iacocca, were setting production limits at 20 percent and 10 percent of the industry, outsourcing up to 70 percent of their parts on competitive bids
to improve quality, and reaching workable accords with
their unions leading to 50 percent reductions in unit production costs, General Motors took on the Saturn project,
acquired EDS and Hughes Aircraft in an effort to create a
mega-organization of technological synergism, moved up
to 80 percent in sourcing of parts and could achieve union
cooperation only with respect to new quality standards in
their small car plants. In winter 1988, GM announced a
new sweeping reorganization in which the five car divisions
merged into two, Buick-Olds-Cadillac and Chevy-Pontiac-
Canada, while it continued having the highest unit production costs in the industry.

GM's managers are not dumb, but they have only one behav-
iorial genetic imprint to work with or guide their change efforts.
Toffler states it even more succinctly. He writes that senior managers can intellectualize the changes that are needed to attain a
third wave environment but cannot do it themselves because
they have a lifetime invested in second wave theory and methods. The issue, then, is how clients in their maturity stage can
be helped to recognize the approaching decline stage, achieve
acceptance, and accomplish rebirth and renewal with new
Champions at the helm. The differences in managerial approach
between the Housekeepers and the Champions are many.

Housekeepers	**Champions**
U.S.-based local and regional markets	Global markets, often skipping local ones
Proprietary sales and distribution	Creative partnership agreements
Mechanistic systems based on "make it now, fix-it-later"	Simple systems that work well the first time with lower error rates
Top-down management structures	Team management and consensus
Heavy emphasis on midlevel management control of everything	Flat structures with few middle managers
Heavy emphasis on short-term profits above all else	Balanced emphasis on current earning and reinvestment in future earnings
Heavy emphasis on postsales engineering service to fix problems	Emphasis on quality to avoid problems at outset
Long runs to maximize efficiency	Short, batched runs with customer input
Heavy capital investments so "bigger is better"	Minimized capital investments through partnerships, networking, and outsourcing
Vertical integration and high vulnerability to change	Horizontal mobility and great flexibility

11

Further, the ills faced by Housekeeper managers fall into three general areas. The first has to do with developmental approaches, systems, equipment, facilities, and products. The Europeans and the Japanese today are taking more of an organic approach to their markets with the goal of designing their system or product as close to fail-safe as possible the first time so that it works well and goes on working well, for years. This leads to customer expectations being met or surpassed. Some people call it Quality Engineering or QE. The large American firms used to be good at QE, too, before they matured and became machine bureaucracies. In the 1940s, especially, they tended to overdesign everything. But after World War II, basic U.S. industries matured within a decade. Organizations emerged based on control, change was stifled, while the prevalent thinking in these mechanistic organizations went something like this: with unlimited resources, you can solve any problem. For example, you can design your system quickly. If you throw a lot of resources at it, it has a good chance of turning out well. If it becomes problematic, just throw more resources at it to fix whatever is wrong. If the product is faulty coming off the line, sell it anyway. We can always fix it later if and when a customer complains. It's too expensive to stop the line and fix what's broken. But over time, this style of management is doomed to fail because it develops products that don't work or fall apart. All the postsales service in the world won't convince customers to buy your wares a second time if they have had a bad experience before and can find alternatives. Mechanistic management is also notoriously expensive. It is the mother of all those systems that require $2X$ number of personnel to operate them: X number to actually operate the system and an equal number of people to devote their time to correcting the inherent errors in the system as it was designed. This, for example, explains all the hundreds of people one finds in the back offices of banks and insurance companies running their administrative systems.

As long as the United States had access to unlimited resources and consumers had few alternatives, the Housekeepers appeared successful, and methods based on these values seemed to work. But with the oil crunch of the early 1970s coupled with double-digit interest rates and the rampant inflation of the early 1980s, the Housekeepers could no longer cope. Change was required, and change is not a part of their paradigm. In the interim, a number of overseas companies led by the Japanese began marketing QE-developed products as alternatives. The response of the marketplace is history. Compared to the American auto, watch, radio, steel, and stereo markets, General Custer was lucky!

GLOBAL CONCEPTS

A second trend difficult for many American firms to comprehend and deal with, regardless of their organizational life stage, is the recognition that an ever-larger affluent consumer market exists abroad that, because of its education level, social sophistication, and buying power, is universal in its discretionary spending habits. About the only thing differentiating it is geography and language. As a result, luxury and convenience products from Turbo Porsches and Rolex watches to Mount Blanc fountain pens and Gucci loafers sell as well in Rio and Singapore as they do in New York, Paris, or Tokyo. The implication is that if a firm has a quality consumer product, it is probably marketable on a global basis. Yet few American companies know how to market globally or even consider it as a strategic alternative. A more typical response is, "Milan? How can I think about selling my widgets in Milan when I don't even have a distributor for Chicago?" The question that really should be asked is, "Why go up against seven other American widget makers in the Chicago market when widgets are virtually unknown in Milan?" It is this concept of constrained, concentric geographic marketing— with Omaha logically following Denver, and then Chicago and Louisville, leading to Philadelphia, Atlanta, and Boston—that restricts the potential of many American products and the success of their manufacturers. A tangential issue here, of course, is the aversion of American managers for the apparent complexity of international letters of credit, something most Japanese and Europeans master in high school.

13

GLOBAL COMPETITION

The third issue that bedevils American managers is international marketing as it is carried out by the few firms that do try to export. The typical mechanistic approach is to start from scratch, build a captive salesforce or distribution network, and then market the product. Internationally this compulsion to control everything is so costly and time consuming that, with Americans anyway, xenophobia sets in. The differences in customs, values, and language make Americans terribly insecure abroad. We tend to believe that anyone who cannot speak English is out to fleece us; or with equally bizarre logic, that anyone who can speak fluent English should be trusted. In research performed a few years ago by an international consulting firm, a number of smaller American-based high technology companies were asked whether they marketed their products overseas and, if so, whether they were satisfied with their overseas marketing results. The majority of those queried stated that, yes, they did try to market their high tech products abroad but, no, they were not satisfied with their foreign wholesale agents and distributors. In just about every case, those people were chosen quickly, usually on the basis of their being fluent in English. Seldom were critical distribution decisions made based on references, reputation, track record, and other typical performance-based criteria that would have been used in the United States to make similar local determinations.

When reviewing successful international firms and their global marketing tactics, we find not captive sales or distribution systems but sophisticated organic partnership agreements. These allow successful European distributors to market American products in return for an American-based captive salesforce marketing some heretofore unknown European product with potential for taking the American market by storm. A tit for a tat, so to speak. And perhaps the only people really able to speak the same language are the lawyers and the consultants on both sides, who are instructed to find ways to make the deal happen, not find ways to kill it.

GLOBAL COMPENSATION

The implications of these facts when taken to their logical conclusions are far-reaching. For U.S. firms to rediscover QE, for example, a good many extant products and many more extant systems must be scrapped. In scrapping them, large numbers of employees who know nothing but a mechanistic approach to work may have to be scrapped, too. Further, to bring operating costs in line with overseas competitors, entire organization structures must be rendered asunder and thousands of midlevel managers released as redundant employees. Tens of thousands more may have to go in the blue-collar ranks as automation replaces rote and clerical work. Finally, local sales and salesforces may not be as important in the future as distribution methods overseas. Stated another way, if a Korean company pays an engineer $30,000 a year to develop and manufacture new toys, then that's all that job is worth anywhere in the world today. A toy engineer in Dallas cannot ask for or hope to get more. If he or she does, then the production costs of that American toy company will be greater than the costs of the Korean toy company. Eventually the U.S. firm will fail and that American engineer will be out of a job. As far-fetched as it all may sound, such forces are in play right now and many American companies, and entire U.S.-based industries, have already felt the pinch.

15

READY, FIRE, AIM!

As one delves deeper into the morass of problems, other more detailed issues surface. Housekeepers believe a firm should maintain large inventories (Just-In-Case), whereas the new Tank Commanders preach proven methods of minimal inventory management systems (Just-In-Time). Mechanistic management philosophy also states that major capital expenditures are necessary for massive outlays of plant and equipment that will justify themselves by making possible long, unitary production runs and other cost-saving manufacturing techniques. Our international competitors have learned how to minimize such capital expenditures by outsourcing as much production as possible. This allows several things to happen. First, it puts tremendous competitive pressures for quality on the subcontractors—one slip and they are replaced. Second, it allows enormous flexibility to move from one process to another virtually overnight, which supports frequent product development and innovation. Third, it allows shorter, batch-type processing and production, allowing customers, in turn, to have more and more frequent input to product specifications, model variations, and so forth. The results of this approach create some very powerful alternatives in the marketplace, alternatives that the marketplace naturally prefers to the Model-T and plain vanilla.

COST MANAGEMENT—A NEW DRIVING FORCE

As we will see in the chapter on strategic management consulting, most of the best minds in business today agree that there are only two ways to approach the marketplace: either by seeking value added, which means top-of-the-line quality, or, more commonly, by seeking to offer the lowest price. To succeed in the vast segment of the marketplace that operates based on price alone, cost containment must be the firm's Key Factor of Success (KFS). Large capital investments and their related levels of depreciation, complex, overstaffed organizations, overpaid, underused middle managers overseeing aggrieved labor performing simple rote tasks—all these spell failure and are no longer permissible. Unfortunately, after decades of Housekeepers in key management positions, many American firms have forgotten the principles of cost containment and have no idea how to compete successfully on price alone.

BIGGER IS NOT ALWAYS BETTER

Following the old paradigm that "bigger is better," American firms in the 1960s and 1970s amassed some of the largest holdings imaginable.

At one point in the early 1970s, under the leadership of Harold Geneen, ITT owned 187 companies in over fifty countries.

Companies like ITT became the Roman Empires of enterprise. Own and control the world! With the genius of hindsight we now know that such approaches don't work well. Whenever managers try to build something that big they tend to fail, because in acquiring so many different businesses, there are few that they understand thoroughly enough to manage well. All the rest become orphans in the stream and decline in their performance relative to their respective industry peers. Over time, senior management becomes disillusioned with such holdings and their disappointing returns, and either spins off such businesses again or shuts them down entirely. Those megacorporations that defer both decisions often become the objects of the likes of T. Boone Pickens and Saul Steinberg, the "greenmail" specialists of the mid-1980s. Such corporate raiders have made fortunes simply by taking over unmanageable conglomerates and selling off fundamentally good but neglected subsidiary companies, companies greatly undervalued in the stock market relative to their book values. An even worse fate awaits those who amass mega-organizations on the basis of vertical integration. Vertical integration can be a very risky proposition because it locks the enterprise and its sister firms into a particular market or industry. What is the company supposed to do when, as often happens nowadays, new technology makes the entire industry obsolete overnight?

18

DEREGULATION—A BARREL OF FUN

If this is not enough to depress you, other major trends and problems have afflicted various specific industries. Airlines, trucking, banking, and telecommunications, among others, have been deregulated in comparatively short time spans after decades of tight or total government regulation. When the government decided to deregulate the airline industry, it had hoped to increase competition, especially on major routes, to the benefit of air travelers. In fact, the frequent air traveler has been hurt more by deregulation than anyone could ever have imagined. By allowing virtually unlimited flights by an unlimited number of carriers, major air terminals today are log-jammed, delays are the rule not the exception, and the only price discounts available are for infrequent fliers on holiday, not frequent commercial travelers. The major airlines have moved in and acquired many of the successful trunk airlines such as Air California and PSA, immediately doubling or tripling regional fares to offset their discounts to tourists and students on national routes. At the same time, many cities that had government-protected air service now have infrequent flights, if any. The alternative is to take a bus—if Trailways hasn't closed the local depot.

FIBER OPTICS, ANYONE?

The deregulation of the telephone company was equally disastrous for different reasons. In this case, the government, in its infinite wisdom, insisted that AT&T have a full complement of competitors so that, in theory at least, users could opt for different equipment makers and line companies and, through free and open markets, costs would come down. However, Congress completely forgot about the concept of "cost of entry." As a result, although it was made much more complex and costly for AT&T and its various units to operate, no real competitors have been able to wrestle major market share away from 'Ma Bell'. The result has been a steep increase in telephone costs for average users and a steep decline in the quality of service.

19

A TEDDY BEAR WITH EVERY CAR LOAN

Perhaps the most classic industry deregulation, with some of the most predictable results, has been that of financial services, and banking in particular. For the better part of fifty years, the government dictated to this industry what rates would be charged for loans, paid on deposits, earned on interest margin, and so forth. Further, the government dictated what ancillary businesses bankers could enter, and local regulators controlled where bankers could do business and if they could do it at all in a given locale. Of course, the nearsightedness of this approach was that such controls applied only to enterprises that both accepted deposits and made loans and thus earned the label *bank*.

Beginning in the early 1970s, and at an exponential growth rate thereafter, a number of firms led by growth-oriented Tank Commanders saw the profits to be made by being in the business of money lending. They also learned that as long as they did not raise their funds through accepting deposits, they could circumvent the banking regulations and run competitive circles around banks and thrift institutions. For a while, they did just that. The reaction of the banking community, of course, was first denial, then bargaining with "big brother" to put these upstarts out of business. Instead, Congress decided to deregulate the banks so that they could compete with the upstarts. The consumer, once again, would benefit. In this case, surprisingly, the consumer *has* benefited enormously. As major car manufacturers expanded their consumer credit subsidiaries, they offered rates as low as 2.5 percent on new car financing. Other nonbank firms such as American Express have developed their own credit capabilities, while banks have entered the discount brokerage and insurance areas.

It has been, however, a tragically painful transition for the banking industry. After fifty years of government protection and Housekeeper management, few, if any, banking executives knew how to compete in open market conditions at the moment of deregulation. There was little in the way of productivity built into bank organizations, and bankers steeped in mechanistic management theory knew even less about product development, merchandising or marketing—other than waiting for customers to wander into their offices between 10 A.M. and 3 P.M. Over the ensuing six to eight years following deregulation, we saw a coalescing of the industry, the development of a totally new paradigm of bank management principles and values, and a host of entrepreneurial, organically managed newcomers, all generating new products and services, sometimes without the fees and charges traditionally levied by bankers. Having lost out in major market segments such as new car financing, and with traditional profit areas such as agricultural and petrochemical lending failing them, bankers sought desperately to find new sources of revenue and reduce their previously extravagant operating expenses. What has emerged are some gigantic regional banking organizations such as Key Banks and Carteret Savings in the Northeast, Citizens & Southern in the Southeast, and BancOne in the Midwest. There also has been tragedy and monumental failure, especially in the savings and loan industry. During regulation particularly strong management was never needed, and thus senior thrift management was totally unprepared to cope in a deregulated marketplace. So many major savings institutions are bankrupt that the federal insurance fund supporting them is virtually bankrupt, too, and failed S&Ls cannot be closed down as they should be. Instead, the government allows them to continue, in limbo, hoping there won't be a run on deposits and constantly putting off some hard decisions.

HARD ISSUES AND EASY SOLUTIONS

Given all this, is it any wonder that for the past twenty years, mechanistic managers have been looking for quick, easy solutions? One can stand only so much pain. Further, the mechanistic school of management states that solutions should be quick and easy. Just throw more resources into the conflagration! You say Quality Circles get employees involved and reduce dissatisfaction? That's swell. Let's start a dozen first thing tomorrow morning! Management-By-Walking-Around brings managers closer to the business? Terrific! Let's have all plant managers on a MBWA schedule by next week. Management-By-Objectives helps employees learn how to plan and accept responsibility for their actions? Super! Let's put all 2,000 supervisory personnel on MBO starting next quarter. The regulatory authorities are insisting that all savings and loans submit a documented five-year business plan? Well, call up a consultant and have him draw one up for us and send it in. Now, can I get back to redrawing the organization chart to improve control?

Mechanistic management has failed American executives completely. It has created false expectations and reinforced our xenophobia to the point where managers have trouble learning a better way to do things. For all these reasons, management consultants have more responsibility to their clients than ever before. The problem is that far too many consultants themselves were raised on mechanistic management principles and still try to apply them to every kind of problem today. But these second wave solutions are not going to resolve third wave issues. Instead, what clients need—and what consultants must deliver— is a much more sophisticated approach, one that addresses decline and denial and helps clients reach acceptance quickly so that they can attain rebirth and renewal, develop effective global marketing strategies, and relearn cost containment principles and organizational flexibility.

Such approaches are not easy for consultants to teach or managers to learn. They require a great deal of patience, time, experimentation, and, yes, money. Every step of the way, consultants face that genetically implanted, mechanistic resistance to change, an inability to perceive consulting fees as anything other than a current operating expense, and the ingrained paradigm of control-based management. It is unfortunate that a significant number of managers now at the peak of their careers continue to follow the old paradigm in the last years of this century. At last, however, many are realizing that the old methods and values aren't working the way they used to. One result of this realization is that the consulting industry shifted from rapid expansion in the 1970s to explosive growth in the 1980s.

RECOMMENDED READINGS

Block, P., *The Empowered Manager* (San Francisco: Jossey-Bass, 1987).

Davis, S.M., *Future Perfect* (Reading, Mass.: Addison-Wesley, 1987).

Drucker, P., *Innovation and Entrepreneurship: Practice and Principles* (New York: Harper & Row, 1985).

Gilbreath, R. D., *Forward Thinking* (New York: McGraw-Hill, 1987).

Goldsmith, W., and D. Clutterbuck, "The Losing Streak," *New Management* 2 (2) (1984).

Goodman, S. T., *How to Manage a Turnaround* (New York: The Free Press, 1984).

Hall, W. K., "Survival Strategies in a Hostile Environment," *Harvard Business Review* (Sept.-Oct. 1980).

Mintzberg, H., *Structures in Fives: Designing Effective Organizations* (Englewood Cliffs, N. J.: Prentice-Hall, 1983).

Otis, I., "Observations of the Japanese Automotive Industry: A Lesson for American Managers," *IM Magazine* (May-June 1987).

O'Toole, J., "Why Good Companies Get into Trouble," *New Management* 4, (1) (Summer 1986).

————, *Vanguard Management* (New York: Doubleday, 1985).

Pascale, R. T. and A. G. Athos, *The Art of Japanese Management* (New York: Warner Books, 1981).

Peters, T., "A World Turned Upside Down," *Academy of Management Executive* (August 1987).

Peters, T. and R. H. Waterman, *In Search of Excellence* (New York: Warner Books, 1982).

Porter, M. E., *Competitive Advantage: Creating and Sustaining Superior Performance* (New York: The Free Press, 1985).

Steiner, G. A., *The New CEO* (New York: Macmillan, 1983).

Toffler, A., *The Third Wave* (New York: William Morrow & Co., 1980).

23

CHAPTER 2

AN
INDUSTRY
COMES
OF
AGE

As the framework of management shifts, so does the framework of consulting, putting new pressures and demands on management consultants. We are now seeing major changes both in the consulting services demanded by clients and in the major consulting firms providing those services; and these changes are taking place in the context of the relentless, almost frenzied, growth of the consulting industry. There are five key trends that are changing the profession and creating a new paradigm of consulting:

- Expansion of demand for consulting services,
- Increased specialization of services provided,
- Internationalization of the consulting industry,
- Consolidation of medium and large firms,
- Increased dominance of university-based independents.

We will look at each of these trends and their implications for consultants in this chapter.

GROWTH AND EXPANSION

Of all the growth in the past few years, the most spectacular has been among the "Big-8" accounting firms. Organizations such as Arthur Andersen, Peat Marwick Main & Co., Ernst & Whinney, Coopers and Lybrand, and Arthur Young have doubled, and in some cases trebled, their "management services" or consultant billings to the point where Big-8 firms represent half of the ten largest consulting organizations in the world. In fact, the largest management consultancy in the world is Arthur Andersen (AA). This is remarkable because the firm specializes in systems and data processing consulting and turns away most other requests for nonaudit assistance. AA employs more than 8,000 professionals worldwide and annual billings now exceed $750 million. The practice has doubled every five years since its inception over thirty-five years ago, for an annual growth rate of 15 percent. The firm's 1986 billings grew more than 30 percent over 1985 receipts. Although Arthur Andersen is an extraordinary example of the success of the Big-8 accounting firms, several others are billing annual consulting fees in the hundreds of millions, too. Several of these giant worldwide accounting firms now realize consulting fees in excess of audit fees. It is safe to say that annual Big-8 consulting fees exceeded $2.5 billion in 1987, and the latest figures available for the industry are out of date already (see Table 2–1).

McKinsey & Company, Temple Barker & Sloane, A. T. Kearney, Management Analysis Center (MAC), Stanford Research Institute, and many other major consulting organizations, have grown rapidly during this same period. The best estimate of total U.S. and worldwide consulting fees in 1982-83 were $2.5 and $5 billion, respectively. Today these figures have more than doubled, and U.S.-based billings now exceed $6 billion, while worldwide the profession is generating fees of more than $12 billion annually. At this rate of growth, AA alone soon will have annual billings in excess of $1 billion. Some would argue that not all of AA's thousands of programmers constitute true "consulting," any more than do Booz, Allen's defense contract work or A. T. Kearney's logistics software services, but proprietary products and services do make up a major portion of billings in the industry and will continue to do so into the next decades.

A major source for the industry's continued growth in the United States is the expansion of the largest firms into new, regional markets such as the Southeast, and the growth of smaller, local firms into regional organizations, some of which now threaten the traditional markets of the largest firms. Theodore Barry & Associates (TBA) struggled unsuccessfully for a number of years trying to become a major international firm; more recently it has concentrated its efforts in the Southwest and has become a major player in the engineering and technical manufacturing consulting markets, often winning contracts from larger rivals. Kibel & Green, originally known as Alpha-Omega,

TABLE 2.1

**Largest Management Consulting Practices
in Fees Billed as of December 31, 1986***

	Fees Billed (in millions)
Arthur Andersen[a]	$640
McKinsey & Company	400
Towers, Perrin, Forster, and Crosby	370
Mercer Meidinger[b]	360
Peat Marwick Main & Co.[a]	340
Booz, Allen & Hamilton	340
Coopers & Lybrand[a]	305
Ernst & Whinney[a]	280
Wyatt	270
Arthur Young[a]	200
Bain & Co.	200

a. Member of a Big-8 accounting firm.
b. Subsidiary of Marsh & McLennan, Inc.
*Source: *The Economist,* 2/13/88

has grown rapidly, too, to become a major firm serving troubled companies all along the West Coast, while The Warner Group has begun to challenge AA for major systems contracts. These are typical of dozens of successful firms that have concentrated their marketing efforts to dominate the market niches they serve. Cambridge Energy Research Associates (CERA) specializes in providing technical information on petrochemical markets and supplies to clients worldwide. The firm has grown tenfold in the past five years. Additionally, new practices and partnerships are springing up all the time. Jim Kennedy's *Directory of Management Consultants,* although the best available reference book, is only as complete and accurate as the data the industry sends Kennedy; he does not actively seek out firms to include. Invariably, the directory is larger each time it is published, but at least one firm is missing for every firm listed. For example, a recent issue of *Modern Healthcare* published a list of over 220 consulting firms that claim to specialize in serving that industry. Fewer than half are found in Kennedy's directory.

FROM MANAGER TO CONSULTANT

Perhaps one of the greatest impetuses for growth among the independent firms has been the trend in U.S. industry to retire more managers prematurely in order to flatten the structure, facilitate communications, and reduce costs. I have observed this phenomenon as secretary of my Harvard Business School class. Over the past four or five years, more than a third of the class has "retired." Many of us are not even gray yet; we are, in fact, in the prime of our managerial lives. These retirees have notified the Alumni Office that they have established a consulting practice, usually to provide services back to their former industries. This experience is not an aberration: It is occurring with greater frequency throughout the country.

In the space of eighteen months, Wells Fargo acquired Crocker Bank in San Francisco, and in consolidating, laid off 2,000 people in the bay area while Bank of America released more than 9,000 people in 1986 and early 1987 in its efforts to regain profitability. They say there are now more than 3,000 banking consultants in San Francisco!

Further, many of these newly created independents are making it and making it big. The years in which they gained industry specialization and experience coupled with their maturity makes them highly attractive to smaller firms in the same industry that cannot afford them as full-time executives but are willing to use them as much as possible on a consultant basis. They provide the experience not held by those in small, entrepreneurial companies. These fledgling practices and partnerships also recognize that networking among independents creates great synergy. Networking allows one small consulting partnership to offer clients a broad range of services. Such loose affiliations also can generate business for all members of the network as each markets services based on the needs of clients and prospects. Although this may have been difficult to realize in earlier decades, when consultants typically tended to tell prospects that they could do anything so as to keep as much business as possible for themselves, today specialization brings a new honesty. Because more firms are specializing more narrowly, they are willing to market for one another with less suspicion and a greater sense of reciprocity.

SPECIALTIES AND SPECIALISTS

As the need for organizational rebirth and renewal becomes more acute, and as a greater number of specific industries face their own unique sets of problems, specialized industry-oriented knowledge has become fundamental in gaining clients. This is true in the financial services industry, the airline and health services industries, the communications and defense industries, the pharmaceutical and retail foods industries, and a good number of others. Further, U.S.-based manufacturers, in markets that are rapidly slipping away from this country, increasingly want to know whether the consultants have dealt with other, similar problems of global competition. In short, a major piece of the emerging paradigm is specialization in specific industry issues: key factors of success, external threats, technology applications, international market opportunities, and so forth. In fact we are seeing the consulting profession move through a continuum as firms progress from being all things to all people, to orchestrated specialties, to technical specialists with process skills. At least this appears to be the direction successful firms, both large and small, are taking.

There is no question that a major reason for Arthur Andersen's unparalleled success has been the firm's decision some fifteen years ago to concentrate solely in systems work. Almost all of the other Big-8 firms are more general in their management services approach or have developed specialist SWAT teams serving specific industries and requiring unique knowledge and expertise. AA passed up the opportunity to be "all things to all people" and became *the* systems firm—expert in systems as they apply to all industries and not expert in any one industry. The gamble has more than paid off, for Arthur Andersen can do things no one else can. For example, the firm has a centralized service that monitors the development of software all over the world. If a given kind of software exists, AA is probably aware of it or can run it down quickly. By specializing as it has, AA has become one of the largest information service businesses in the world, along with EDS and IBM.

Other firms have become nationally recognized for their specialization efforts, too. Kaplan, Smith began serving the savings and loan industry in 1980 out of a Washington, D.C., office, performing financial analyses and stock conversion assistance. The firm now has additional offices on the West Coast and has become an important resource for the financial services industry in financial management and general consulting services. Spicer & Oppenheimer provides specialist services to the international investment banking community, while Senn-Delaney Associates, specialists in management education and development, began in Long Beach, California, and moved in the opposite direction. It now has offices as far east as Chicago.

We are witnessing both new growth in old specialties (such as training and development, as they can be applicable to clients attempting renewal) and the emergence of new specialties (based on technology, its transfer, and and its applications in specific industries). This phenomenon is particularly true wherever there has been enormous change requiring the support of training or new kinds of compensation, especially in response to rapid deregulation. Government, too, is changing the type of consultant it hires. Because of the specificity of government organization and job requirements, government agencies traditionally have hired only consultants with great technical expertise. Today, government organizations are increasingly hiring process specialists who are experts in government and how it works.

31

GLOBAL CONSULTING

The third major aspect of the consulting industry's new paradigm is the phenomenon of global markets and global competition. This factor has begun to affect consulting firms as much as it affects client organizations. The entry of major players (such as the British firm of Saatchi & Saatchi and its U.S.-based acquisitions such as Hay & Associates and Cleveland Consulting Associates) together with the expansion of the U.S. offices of international firms (such as Egon Zender & Associates out of Switzerland, the PA Consulting Group from England, C.A.S.T. Management Consultants from Milan, and Kienbaum & Associates out of Germany) are harbingers of what I believe has just begun: a major invasion of the U.S. consulting market by European firms. Some of the largest in England, Germany, and Scandinavia have not arrived yet, but their appearance here is only a matter of time. In 1986, the British Management Consultancies Association—an industry affiliation of twenty-five major firms estimated to account for approximately 50 percent of all consultant billings in Britain—reported that the United States represented 30 percent of the British "foreign" market, presenting the greatest overseas growth potential for British consulting firms. Further, in interviews with the managing directors of top consulting organizations in London, British managers bragged openly that in their estimation, honors graduates from Oxford and Cambridge Universities were far more well-rounded and analytical than Harvard or Wharton M.B.A.s and represented a talent edge in international market penetration. As more and more British clients find "bargains" in U.S. acquisitions or develop international agreements and affiliations with American companies, these British consulting firms will be asked to do more for the new, U.S.-based affiliates of their clients. Conversely, U.S. firms such as A.T. Kearney (the largest U.S. consulting firm abroad), McKinsey & Co., Booz, Allen, and Temple, Barker & Sloane and Big-8 partnerships such as Arthur Andersen, Ernst & Whinney and Peat Marwick Main, under its English aegis of Peat Marwick & McClintock, are rapidly expanding their international efforts, helping clients develop the networks they need to market and distribute products and technologies worldwide within the concept of global markets and competition as it exists today. Towers, Perrin, Forster, and Crosby, for example, has seen a 40 percent increase in compensation work out of its London office in just the last three years. These changes, too, form a continuum, as international firms move from having separate offices in each country (much like Big-8 offices in the United States), to "global practices" in which projects are staffed from many offices and roving teams of consultants provide integrated staff support to major international projects wherever they are needed.

There are a number of smaller, medium-sized firms, such as Handley-Walker Company and ECOTEC based in England, that are growing rapidly to become major international firms, too.

Other British firms, such as PE International and Inbucon, are merging to create even larger competitive entities. Perhaps this is one motivation for the recent acquisition of Alexander Proudfoot by a large U.K. pension firm. If the market in the United States is growing at a 15 percent per year pace, then it would seem that the international consulting market is expanding at that rate and perhaps more. Again, one of the principal problems is a lack of centralized, volunteered data. No players in this arena want to let competitors know they are coming.

CONSOLIDATION OF LARGE CONSULTING FIRMS

At the same time all this growth has been taking place, there also has been some consolidation. World-renowned firms such as Temple, Barker & Sloane and Mercer Meidinger have been acquired by companies outside the industry (both by the insurance brokerage firm of Marsh & McLennan), while others such as Cresap, McCormick & Padget have been acquired by still larger consulting firms (Towers, Perrin, Forster, and Crosby). Others, such as the nationally recognized firms of Barry & Company and Jameson & Associates, have failed outright, while still others, such as Booz, Allen and MAC, have closed some offices in major markets. Even the apparent paragons of success, such as Arthur D. Little, have seen earnings in the mid-1980s level out or fall to levels no greater than those realized a decade before. Perhaps this explains the attempted take over of ADL in mid-1987 by Plenum, a printing firm.

What's behind this consolidation and "shrinkage" at a time when a large part of the industry is experiencing continued, unbounded growth? I believe much of this contradiction rests with individual firms and their strategic objectives. The largest require capital to expand internationally, to avoid having their

Fortune 500 clients be better served by more globally placed firms. Others still must face up to their inability to change with the times, to meet more demanding client needs, and to meet the external threats to those clients' industries. As will be discussed in detail later in the book, firms that continue to deliver mechanistic management values to clients in need of new, more organic approaches will eventually lose out. Many of the most successful consulting firms in the 1960s and 1970s built their practices off the "content" approach—in which the role of the consultant was to diagnose the problem, *tell* the client how to solve it, and then lead or even perform the remedial actions. But many clients, in their efforts to deploy assets and develop new corporate values, have either developed internal consulting capabilities or demand a different role from their external consultants, something more akin to process consulting. The largest firms practicing the process approach get clients thoroughly involved in all stages of a project—from identifying problems to developing and implementing solutions—using project teams with staff from both the client and the consulting organizations. Often these relationships become so close that the client naturally continues to work with the same consulting firm, instead of putting later phases of the project out for a new bid. Thus, for firms that can offer it, process consulting provides a competitive advantage, and those firms unwilling or unable to change their approach didn't perform well in the early 1980s.

A secondary problem that the consulting industry would appear to have—one not unknown in most other industries—is a lack of leadership. I spoke recently with the senior management of several firms that had been forced to close some of their offices. I found that the main reason they were forced to do so was their inability to find or replace the kind of experienced consultants, managers, and partners who could aggressively market and act as leaders to the local staff. Although there are plenty of consultants about, the leadership ability required to sell business and manage an office while developing younger consultants seems to be rare.

Amid all this simultaneous (and apparently contradictory) expansion and contraction of consulting practices, some firms are actively seeking to acquire others whose specialties are in great demand and merge these unique practices into "a firm of many firms." Saatchi & Saatchi has done this with some success internationally in the advertising field and now appears to be trying the same approach in the consulting profession. Peat Marwick Main, now second only to AA among the Big-8 consulting practices, has acquired or formed strategic alliances with over half a dozen other leading firms including Nolan Norton, Alex Sheshunoff, and Golembe & Associates. Towers, Perrin, Forster, and Crosby has also acquired several key firms including Cresap. If synergies are to be gained by such a concentration of talents, we will probably see the trend continue. But if such combined firms fail to hold the individual entrepreneurs who founded the specialty practices, then it will have been, at best, an expensive experiment.

35

THE ACADEMIC INDEPENDENT

Amid all this change, expansion, and contraction, there is a new segment of the industry that is growing equally fast. Simply described, it is the emergence of the academic independent—business school professors armed not with academic theories but with practical know-how, action research, and a mastery of process skills and capable of translating complex academic and organizational theory into easily understandable and usable advice. These academic independents represent another apparent contradiction in the industry. After all, process consultation is very nonspecific. In its purest, Socratic form it provides the client with little direct advice at all. Yet nonspecific advice is precisely the kind of assistance companies need in their renewal efforts. At the same time, while clients recognize the value of nonspecific counsel, it must be applicable to the specific parameters of their industry and its problems.

Most of these academic independents work out of their offices in universities or out of their homes so that they have no real overhead to pass on to their clients. A good number of these academic professionals are associated with leading research centers such as the Center for Effective Organization (CEO) at U.S.C. and Kilmer's management development shop. Further, all of these academic independents network within their own business schools and nationally within their academic disciplines. The result is that these university-based consultants are capable of helping even very large clients by subcontracting through their networks.

■CASE IN POINT

Professor Alan Glassman is one of the leading consultants nationally in government processes and administration, and works with federal, state, and local government organizations. In a recent project, which ran for five years, Alan subcontracted with more than a dozen other consultants and academics, each a specialist in his or her own field, and maintained quality control and project scheduling and management for the client.

This new breed of independent is capable of capturing an ever-larger share of the market for midsized and smaller client companies, enterprises that require strong industry specialization coupled with the process skills attainable only through years of study, research, and application in that particular industry.

Fortune 1,000 employment levels have not changed in the past twenty years, nor are they forecast to change much in the next twenty years. Rather, the greatest growth in our economy has been, and will continue to be, the midsized and smaller companies with fewer than 100 employees. Academic independents may become the most powerful of all consultants over the next decade or two. They represent the real growth sector of the consulting profession. At one end of the consulting industry, the largest firms are getting larger through mergers and acquisitions while serving *Fortune* 500 companies primarily; while at the other end, there are hundreds of small, independent, highly-specialized practices that are becoming ever more important as they fill niches in the marketplace for all manner of clients. At the same time, academic independents and industry specialists retired early from *Fortune* 500 firms are providing the technical and process needs at the growth end of the economy at reasonable cost and with almost no overhead. These academic independents and industry experts have none of the concerns that used to be felt by independent consultants who believed that what they do and how they do it is unique. Instead, they thrive on networking, affiliation, and knowledge-sharing and enjoy all the advantages such activities bring.

37

It is the consulting firms in the middle ground that are being hurt by these developments. They are still too small or too regional to be on the RFP lists of the *Fortune* 500, and their organizations are filled with older consultants steeped in obsolete content skills and generalist attitudes—products, if you will, of outdated management values based on concepts of control and uniformity. We come to the same apparent contradiction: an industry that is growing in enormous leaps and bounds at a time of consolidation and failure. This general picture, however, is common in many industries. Michael Porter has taught American business that it must either be the lowest-cost provider or deliver a perceived value added and charge the highest price. To fall in the middle is certain death. As consultants should know better than anyone, the same principle applies to them.

CONSOLIDATION OF INDUSTRY ORGANIZATIONS

A few years ago there were more than a half dozen affiliations for consultants to join. Today there are only three for full-time consultants and one for academic independents consulting part-time or teaching consulting skills. All the other organizations have merged or failed. The only organization for independent consultants, small firms, and partnerships today is the *Institute of Management Consultants* (IMC). The IMC has more than doubled in size since 1985 and has absorbed several earlier efforts at developing a national training and accreditation body. It provides a series of workshops almost monthly throughout the country for independent, beginning consultants. With its local chapters and loyal supporters, it aggressively screens applicants seeking the certification of Certified Management Consultant (CMC). The IMC now accepts affiliate members, academics and like professional people, who consult on a part-time basis and is developing a nationally acceptable series of examinations for a more broadly recognized CMC accreditation. Further, the IMC publishes *The Journal of Management Consulting*, the only non-academic publication for practicing consultants.

Merged into the IMC in 1987 were the *Association of Management Consultants* (AMC) and the Society of Professional Management Consultants (SPMC), organizations designed to serve consulting firm managers. Its aim continues to be that of "helping principals of management consulting firms to achieve maximum results" under the IMC aegis. The IMC has also become a charter member of the *International Council of Management Consulting Institutes* (ICMCI) whose members include all organizations that certify management consultants worldwide. The ICMCI is working to establish a worldwide reciprocity of certification among its members.

38

The *Management Services Division* of the AICPA (the *American Institute of Certified Public Accountants*, but almost always referred to by its abbreviation), exists expressly to monitor and control the consulting activities of the Big-8 and other major accounting firms. The AICPA recently began the basic work required to develop national testing of Big-8 consultants to assure their capabilities and expertise, much as the AICPA does for its auditors, accountants, and tax experts. There is hope that there will be a close collaboration with the IMC so that a uniform accreditation with instant recognition among the profession and clients can be achieved.

ACME (founded in 1929 as the *Association of Consulting Management Engineers* but now universally and legally called ACME) has not stood still either. As the body for the largest of the pure consulting firms, ACME continues to be a major sounding board for ethics and policy in the industry. Its membership has changed radically over the past two decades. Fully half of the forty-odd firms that constituted ACME membership in 1970 are no longer in business, while another eight to ten have resigned their membership so that over 75 percent of ACME's current 60-firm constituency is new. However, ACME has grown to the point where even the last of the major hold-outs, including McKinsey & Co., are considering active membership. The association is working hard developing and expanding its training programs, seminars, and surveys for member firms. The association also publishes a bi-annual *Annotated Bibliography on Management Consulting*. At this time, nonmembership in ACME by any large consulting firm should be an embarrassment for the firm, not for ACME.

The *Management Consultancy Division* of the *Academy of Management* is the fourth major affiliation for consultants. It is comprised of nearly 1,000 academics who either teach management consulting skills in business schools and in five-year accounting programs or are practicing consultants in their time

39

away from teaching. These individuals serve a much broader field than the IMC.

> ■ CASE IN POINT
> At a recent Academy of Management national conference, I was asked to give a one-day preconference workshop on "Building Your Own Practice." Nearly 100 academics attended, but along with professors of policy, marketing, and finance were physicians from the National Institute of Mental Health, professors of education, psychologists, and many others interested in learning how to market their knowledge to organizations and institutions .

40

It is here, within the Academy of Management, that much of the research on the industry—its growth, services, and requirements—has been performed over the past decade. For example, scholars have explored the effectiveness of outside consultants who aid the strategic planning process. Conclusions emerging from that research include strong evidence that outside consultants have helped to neutralize internal politics in the planning process, provided more detailed and better data with which to plan, and allowed companies to perform more effective external environmental scanning. On the other hand, these researchers found that a large number of firms will not accept the expense of including external consultants in the strategic planning process because they feel that they must invest in short-term issues rather than in long-range thinking about problems that may never occur. Further, as more and more members of the academy leave education to establish full-time management consulting practices, the Management Consultancy Division is taking on a unique profile. With a large national conference annually and a number of regional conferences throughout the year, the division is becoming a major intellectual complement to the IMC for any consultant who has a legitimate connection with higher education. Perhaps this is one reason that the division created nonvoting Executive Committee memberships for members of both ACME and the IMC. Finally, although not connected in any way with the Academy of Management, *Consultation* is a quarterly journal devoted to publishing the practical aspects of academic research with respect to the consulting profession and the consultative process.

DECLINE AND FALL

This brings us full circle. I proposed several years ago that management consulting was, and would continue to be, a dynamic, growth-oriented profession. History has proven this prediction correct. What is important to recognize today, however, is that consulting is not just a profession but an *industry*. Consulting firms rival industrial giants in size and annual revenues, and they play an increasingly dynamic role in world business, strategy, and competition. But there are some dark clouds on the horizon for the unwary. The line is being drawn between the very large, very expensive organizations that exist to assuage the fears of the *Fortune* 1,000, and the growing number of highly skilled and knowledgeable independents who have roots in specific industries or in academia or in both. These independents are capable of providing both industry specialization and process skills to an increasingly demanding clientele. The old consulting skills and approaches that served so well through the 1970s are valid for and acceptable to an ever-shrinking segment of clients. American firms today are primarily interested in cutting-edge assistance in the form of highly targeted, industry-based problem resolution and in consultants well versed in international trade and business networking. They are clients smart enough to figure out their own solutions. What they need are individuals knowledgeable enough to project the right models and ask the right "why not?" and "what if?" questions of them. Those consultants and firms able to perform and deliver these services will do well in the future. Those who hang on to the old paradigm of content solutions, mechanistic 300-page organization and compensation studies, and surrogate management approaches will continue to weaken and eventually fall by the wayside—as many already have.

RECOMMENDED READINGS

Barcus, S. W. and J. W. Wilkinson, *Handbook of Management Consulting Services* (New York: McGraw-Hill, 1986).

Byrne, J. A., "A Specialist Slips into Big League Consulting," *Business Week* (July 27, 1987).

Greene, J., "Specialization Boosts Competition," *Modern Healthcare* (Sept. 25, 1987).

Greiner, L. E. and R. O. Metzger, *Consulting to Management* (Englewood Cliffs, N.J.: Prentice-Hall, 1983).

"Is Booz, Allen Having a Mid-Life Crisis?," *Business Week* (March 9, 1987).

Kennedy, James H., ed., "The Future of Management Consulting," *Consultants News* (1985).

——— "An Analysis of the Management Consulting Business in the U.S. Today," *Consultants News* (1987).

Kishel, G. F. and P. G. Kishel, *Cashing in on the Consulting Boom* (New York: Wiley, 1985).

Kubr, Milan, ed., *Management Consulting: A Guide to the Profession*, 2d ed. (Geneva: International Labor Organization, 1986).

"Management Consulting," ACME (1988). An annotated bibliography of selected resource material.

Merwin, J., "We Don't Learn from Our Clients, We Learn from Each Other," *Forbes* (Oct. 19, 1987).

Metzger, R. O., "The Changing Paradigm of Consulting," *Journal of Management Consulting* 3 (4) (1987).

"Move Over, Arthur," *The Economist* (Nov. 22, 1986).

Noling, M. S. and J. F. Blumenthal, "Gaining Competitive Advantage," *New Management* 3 (2) (Fall 1985).

Perry, N. J., "A Consulting Firm Too Hot to Handle," *Fortune* (April 27, 1987).

Skapinker, Michael, ed., "Management Consultancy: A Survey," *London Financial Times,* (Oct. 26, 1987).

Stevens, M., *The Big Eight* (New York: Macmillan, 1981).

Weinberg, G. M., *The Secrets of Consulting* (New York: Dorset, 1986).

Wolf, W. B., *Management and Consulting: An Introduction to James O. McKinsey* (New York: Cornell University Press, 1978).

CHAPTER 3

NEW
STANDARDS

Perhaps the best place to begin understanding the changes occurring in our industry is to analyze the changes that have been taking place among our clients. Although these organizations may be in decline or struggling with the concepts of rebirth or renewal, individuals within the organizations have become better educated, better read, more experienced, and more aware of consultants and consulting skills. Over the past ten, and especially the last five years, an increasing number of client executives have held M.B.A. degrees. Such managers, even those in smaller, family-owned firms, are skeptical of what consultants can do for them and are setting new standards for consultant performance. The unassailable aura of the consultant's Harvard or Stanford M.B.A. just isn't there anymore.

An increasing number of clients have worked with consultants, which presents three potential problems for any consultant trying to get in the door. Either the previous consultants were so effective that the client has very high expectations; or the previous consultants were horrible and the client is opposed to ever using consultants again; or the previous consultant did an acceptable job in a particular way and now the client expects the next consultant to use exactly the same methodology. In all three of these cases, that next consultant is going to have a very difficult time living up to the client's expectations.

A third challenge for consultants that wasn't present five years ago is the number of books that have come out about consultants and consulting and that have been read with much curiosity by industry executives as well as by consultants. (The book you are now reading will, perhaps, be one more example.) Along with these new publications have come courses at both the undergraduate and graduate levels in dozens of universities and business schools throughout the United States, Canada and England that concentrate on consulting skills and methods. A majority of those attending these courses do not go on to become consultants but use their new knowledge to help them perform unofficially as internal consultants and as managers in screening, evaluating, and hiring external consultants. The sight of a newly minted staff M.B.A. holding forth on Schein's concepts of process consulting and expanding on every point made in a consultant's presentation can drive an experienced consultant to drink. It can make a beginner suicidal.

The past ten years also have seen an enormous growth in organizations such as the OD Network and the American Society of Training and Development (ASTD), which give human resource managers and personnel staff access to a broad array of process consulting methods, tools, and consultants. In the past, academics and practitioners seldom came together to share opinions or listen to each other. But as was pointed out in the previous chapter, there is a new breed of academic in the business schools who is able to translate management theory into practical advice and seeking opportunities to perform action research. On the corporate side, there is a better-educated generation of managers willing to ask questions and seek solutions from outside. Perhaps this explains the extraordinary amount of "shadowing" we see taking place today—in which senior managers build relationships with leading business professors and call on them frequently to sound out new ideas, to clarify problems, and to test potential solutions. This "shadowing" process allows managers to receive objective feedback on their ideas and strategies before they have to put them forth within the organization. The relationships so developed can make it very difficult for an outside consultant to gain a toehold.

MORE DEMANDING CLIENTS

All of the above has combined to make most consulting prospects sophisticated and demanding. In the largest firms, the *Fortune* 500, enormous pressures have been building to establish new, internal consulting groups where there were none before or expand those that do exist. Many of these larger organizations also have begun developing internal OD staff.

These newer specialists are well versed in process approaches to problem solving and act as internal consultants even when they do not belong to any formal internal consulting organization. Certainly, it is less expensive to hire four Harvard M.B.A.s on a full-time basis and use them for several years on a project basis than to pay two to three times as much each year to a Bain or Booz, Allen team for the same service but without the full-time dedication or loyalty. Moreover, many firms now have engineers and other specialists with M.B.A. degrees paid for by company tuition plans. Management is often determined to put these newly won degrees to the test before bringing in "outsiders." After all, an internal engineer with an M.B.A., under the right organization structure, may indeed be more effective on certain issues than an outside consultant who lacks engineering experience or a background in the firm's culture.

47

Most consultants will counter these objections by citing their independence, their experience in a wide variety of business problems, and their objectivity—all of which make them capable of taking a broad view. But the fact remains, it is getting harder each year to just breeze in the boardroom door, wave a Wharton diploma at the client, do a little "soft shoe," and get a $100,000 contract.

WHAT YOU KNOW AND WHO YOU KNOW

Detailed knowledge of a particular industry is rapidly becoming a qualification for today's consultant. The generalist concepts that prevailed at the Harvard Business School throughout the 1950s, 1960s and early 1970s, built on the belief that a well-trained mind can troubleshoot any problem in any industry, is an obsolete concept. There are still firms such as the Boston Consulting Group and McKinsey & Co. that profess that their top M.B.A.s can work on any client account without foreknowledge of the client or the industry, but such claims are becoming weaker each year, if for no other reason than they make these firms appear out of step with the needs of the marketplace.

Examples of the industry-specific expertise required today are everywhere. To be considered useful in the telecommunications industry, for example, you have to know about global communications, fiber optics, and satellite launching opportunities as much as anything else. The banking industry is no longer driven simplistically by the management of interest spreads between loan income and deposit costs but by "off balance sheet" asset management, international securities markets transactions, and how to provide customers with "here and now, anytime, anyhow" services. In the hospital management field, sufficient familiarity with all of the various government regulations surrounding payment standards is required before anyone can advise a health care facility on the maximization of their revenues. No neophyte can help senior management in these issues without several years' experience in those industries.

You can sell a firm just about anything as long as you can show that major competitors have successfully used the same approach.

An additional qualification for consultants today is who they know and with whom they network. There are as many independent consultants and consultants working for small partnerships as working for the largest firms. Their credibility rests heavily on industry contacts, the indirect resources they can call on, and their ability to provide references from satisfied clients— references, in fact, from a number of satisfied clients who have experienced exactly the same problem as the potential client and for whom the consultant has found an innovative solution. Another current reality is that the largest clients are the least likely to tolerate any form of experimentation, especially when it comes to problem solving. For years it was a standing truism

48

in the consulting industry that the easiest sale to a banker was to show him what another banker had bought. As absurd as this sounds, major industrial firms now take this approach to innovation and problem solving, too.

A SHIFT FROM CONTENT TO PROCESS. . .

Nowadays, as we have seen, the traditional content-based consulting approach is no longer readily accepted by many clients. Given the sophistication of most management teams today, it is unrealistic to think that consultants should personally take charge and direct the solution for the client, while educating the client's managers in how this or that problem should be resolved. Such consulting approaches correspond to the old paradigm of mechanistic management.

Rather than being told what to do and led by the hand, clients with advanced management degrees want to use consultants as "change agents" in a process mode, moving from maturity or decline organization stages back to growth.

In some client organizations, the consultant can see that the client is too smart to be taught anything by a content approach. However, outside experts still play a valuable role in assisting a process through to its conclusion. Many strategic planning consultants, for example, are being called on not to formulate strategy but to act as technical experts guiding the planning efforts of the client's own management team. Another example of this new form of process consulting is found in the organization design approach known now as *Self-design*. This is a method for defining corporate and behavioral values, bringing those values to the surface, and then "cascading" them downward throughout an organization so that worker productivity and quality can be positively and permanently improved. In developing a self-design project, the consultant's only role is to coach and guide the employees of the client organization. The organizational values, their formulation and realization in concrete actions, and the resulting organizational changes all must come from within. The consultant, in fact, is essentially an onlooker. And it is just this outside expert or onlooker relationship that today's clients are seeking. This apparent contradiction in terms—in which sometimes the most effective consultants are those who don't "do" anything—makes consulting more dynamic than ever. The industry specialist, familiar with the problems and demands of an industry, knows which questions to ask and who to ask them of, making process consulting particularly helpful to clients who need guidance but who still want to make their own decisions.

...AND BACK AGAIN

At the other extreme, one finds hundreds of disillusioned Housekeepers who bought what I call "hot tub" management. In the late 1970s and early 1980s, Peters and Waterman got everyone excited with *In Search of Excellence* and concepts such as "management by walking around"; the rigor of W. Edward Deming's statistical work was abandoned in lieu of the stampede to Quality Circles; and Mary Kay Cosmetics began the "great hoedown" approach to sales management. I am aware of one consultant who made a good living selling used orange crates as oratory boxes from which managers were expected to exhort their troops to new and greater heights of productivity. At $35 per used orange crate, I can dig it!

The popularity of fads such as these and books like *The One Minute Manager* are nothing more than management's desperate effort to find easy ways to implement change and innovation. Unfortunately these snap-on solutions don't deal with *the contingency principle*: what may be effective in one company is not necessarily effective in another, even in the same industry. Innovation, experimentation, and, yes, some degree of failure are needed to find what's right for Company A, which will not necessarily be right for Company B. Organizational needs and solutions will change even more when we look across cultures, from Oriental to American to European. Worst of all, these snap-on solutions play up to unrealistic and ignorant beliefs that any major change in behavior or values can come easily, cheaply, and quickly. In fact, every study ever performed in this area shows just the opposite. It takes years to get employees and managers to alter their values and behavior. Ford Motor Company needed eight years to achieve its major objectives for line worker participation. Harry Levinson of the Harvard Medical School related to me his great consulting struggle with Bristol-Myers. It took him fifteen years and three generations of senior management before the corporate culture was modified sufficiently to support the avowed corporate values! It took Alan Glassman five years to reorganize and revitalize a relatively small state law enforcement organization.

No small number of managers has tried to implement the general principles of hot tub management hoping they could avoid hard choices and hard work. In such organizations the immediate pressure for short-term results tends to bankrupt the organization's potential for the future, especially its potential for cost-effective employee productivity. Such firms need help realizing that change and renewal are seldom easy and that managers looking for quick fixes are doing more harm than good with their unrealistic demands for instant gratification. Further, such managerial naiveté sets the company up for the unscru-

51

pulous consultant who promises clients whatever they want to hear just to get a contract.

■ CASE IN POINT

Not long ago a colleague of mine from USC, Tom Cummings, and I were asked to work with a major service organization unable over the previous decade to achieve reasonable levels of employee productivity or to make significant cuts in clerical staff. A self-design project was introduced on an experimental basis in four departments with a great deal of success. But the approach required six months and a good deal of retraining. Senior management determined that at this pace, it would take several years to change the corporate culture and that was totally unacceptable because profits had to be improved 15 percent that year. The project was cancelled, everyone went back to the old way of doing things, and profits were improved through cuts in advertising, promotions, new product and systems development, and compensation. Senior management is delighted with the numbers.

CONTENT CONSULTING LIVES—IN CITY HALL

All this does not mean there is no longer any use for content consulting or any need to give directive advice. On the contrary, some of the most successful process consultants are successful precisely because they have competent content specialists on their staff. When a client agrees with what must be done and requests assistance with implementing the consultant's suggestions, the firm can take on a more directive, specialist role. Another market where such specific approaches are required is in consultation to government. Government organizations are still based on the concept of technical expertise and organized in pyramidal style, with most of the authority and responsibility held by relatively few people at the top. These organizations respond well to directive approaches that teach bureaucrats the managerial skills they may not have had an opportunity to learn. Civil service organizations place people in jobs based on what they can do in a particular technical field—police officers, fire fighters, court stenographers, and so forth. In many cases, when these specialists reach lieutenant or fire captain or supervisor, they are lost. As a result, consultants are often best positioned to help such organizations when they, too, take on the role of technical specialists to train or implement new organization and compensation programs. At the same time, this narrow focus, coupled with the increasing inability of government to provide the services with which it is charged, has caused much dissatisfaction with civil servants generally and has suggested to some people that the civil service should be abolished. In such a scenario, governments would be free again to contract some services outside and to recruit and hire general managers to direct the business of government.

NEW METHODOLOGIES

Content consulting certainly is not entirely passé nor is it always inappropriate—especially for the small client with limited sophistication in its management team. Although such firms can't afford large fees, they too need strong direction from "the expert" if they are to survive. *Turnaround* situations also are ideal for a content approach in instances where the consultant is to play the surrogate Lemon Squeezer. But in most cases, today's new standards and challenges are causing consultants to develop a wide range of new methodologies. These will not replace basic skills, but a knowledge of them will increasingly be needed for the consultant who wants to go beyond a certain point in his or her career. For example, companies are more often seeking consultants to act as leaders of *task forces*—small, focused groups of managers and technical specialists assigned to work on a specific issue or problem. Task force teams allow companies to approach renewal, major innovation, or a new business line by drawing on the talents of people from all over the firm. At the same time, management understands that the best leader of a task force session is someone with broad industry knowledge, sharp problem-solving skills, expertise in developing innovative approaches, and proven facilitative skills. An outside consultant is often the best person to play this critical role. In the same way, the general range of skills that we have been calling *process consultation* are invaluable in helping clients accept ownership of their problems, reach the acceptance stage of decline, and develop innovative approaches and solutions to business problems. Process consultation can, on the one hand, help managers adapt new values and management techniques and, on the other, help workers adopt more productive methodologies. Because most of these issues require people to change their beliefs and values, not just learn new technology-based skills, the organic, process approach is far more effective than a content approach.

Negotiation skills are also currently in demand to assist clients in mergers and acquisitions, to resolve interorganizational strife or severe friction between a board of directors and its management team, or to participate in any other situation where two sides require arbitration and an unbiased, knowledgeable arbiter. A consultant also can act as an *expert witness*—someone who provides an objective point of view on a topic of critical importance to the organization, such as the valuation of its assets, the validity of its compensation programs, or the fairness of its "golden parachute" clauses. The expert witness role provides a growing number of opportunities to consultants who are experts in a given field.

TRAINING THE TRAINER

Another new and expanded role for consultants is training internal staff to act as facilitators and trainers themselves. Some large organizations are increasing their use of Organizational Development (OD) specialists or calling on consultants to develop value-driven self-design programs. But we are not seeing nearly enough of such change efforts. It is disturbing to learn that at many companies, large and small, neither management nor employees are working on any significant programs of renewal. The lack of such major programs affects *Fortune* 500 companies even more than smaller, regional firms. When a consultant is faced with an organization with little process competence in its Human Resource Management (HRM) department, the only solution is to ask that management provide a number of motivated, articulate managers who can be trained in the needed skills and can become dedicated to a self-design or similar program for an extended period. As we have seen, any attempt to provide significant change in large organizations requires unbounded patience and systematic effort over years. Their ability to effectively train others in these critical skills places many consultants in high demand today.

NEW CONSULTANTS FOR NEW CLIENTS

I have been discussing how, over the past few years, client firms have become more sophisticated in identifying their own increasingly complex needs and, in turn, more demanding of the consultants they hire. These companies are learning that process-based programs of innovation, such as self-design, can and do create more productive, profitable organizations. In response, they have turned away from the packaged, content-based solutions that prevailed in the past and away from consultants who try to manage the whole show and sell a single approach. Instead, they have hired consultants willing and able to work with them on their own terms.

Yet these new process consultants still need a thorough technical understanding of the industries they serve and a proven track record in doing what they claim they can do. For many consultants, the growth in their clients' knowledge and sophistication has proven just too challenging. It is a lot easier, and far more ego-gratifying, to pontificate on some specific subject and be treated as the expert. In process consultation, on the other hand, the consultant often has no idea where the discussion will lead or what the issues may be—a potentially threatening situation, especially for the beginner. But the marketplace is getting tired of tyros. To repeat the previous and, by-now obvious, conclusion, those consultants who have been unable or unwilling to make the effort to expand their capabilities beyond the glitter of fad management practices and snap-on solutions are falling by the wayside—and will continue to do so.

We're now ready to generate a series of observations about consultants and clients alike, about where we have come from and where we seem to be going:

Mechanistic Management	Organic Management
Clients:	
Naïve, inexperienced	Sophisticated, frequently use consultants
Few advanced degrees in management	Many advanced and technical degrees
Wanted to be led by experts	Want advice from technical specialists
Used consultants to fill staff voids	Seek ways to make use of in-house talent
Sought packaged, easy solutions	Want tailored, realistic solutions
Would accept generalist approach	Want proof of industry experience
Willing to pay for "name" consultants	Want proposals cost justified

56

Mechanistic Management Consultants:	**Organic Management**
Sold content services	Market the process relationship
Hands-on approach	Advisory approach
Lectured and taught "how to"	Ask probing questions, lead task forces and generate new business from process-oriented relationships
Generalist approach to all prospects	Specialize in one industry or discipline
The larger the firm, the better	Many independents in large networks, or multiple specialists in large firms orchestrated by strong principals
Snap-on solutions and pop management	Short on gimmicks, long on expertise
Few credentials required	Specific industry success required
Tried to sell very large projects	Often sell a series of small contracts or develop ongoing process-oriented relationships
Competition from other consultants	Competition from clients themselves

57

Because today's consultants can no longer be all things to all people, they must make a series of strategic decisions about their own careers:

- In which industry or management discipline should I become an "expert"?
- Is there a value in staying with the very largest consulting organizations beyond a certain level of experience?

Furthermore, given the profound shift from one managing and consulting paradigm to another, consultants also must ask:

- How can I stay abreast of the latest management science developments and avoid getting mentally stale?
- What kind of effort will be needed to market myself given the demands of clients now and in the years to come?
- How can I make the transition from second wave to third-wave consultant, from giving content-based, mechanistic solutions to organic, process-based assistance?

For some, these issues will require major career changes; for others, training or a return to academia. Individual consultants could purchase a lot of study time on national education networks such as the International Universal Consortium (formed by the Universities of Maryland, Tennessee and seventeen other accredited schools to deliver courses through satellite networks, video cassette programs and cable TV) before they even come close to the $100,000 per partner per year spent by AA on its consulting staff. In any case, all of us must realize that most of what worked in the past will not work in the future. Consultants in the next decade will spend as much time networking and studying the latest findings in their field or industry as they do with clients. For clients, too, the implication is that consultants may have fewer billable hours and will become correspondingly more expensive, which, in turn, will place ever-greater demands on consultants to justify the costs of the projects and approaches they propose.

But let us take one step at a time. How does the new paradigm of consulting deal with the marketing of professional services? Is it really any different? What could ever replace pounding concrete, knocking on doors, and sending out business development letters?

RECOMMENDED READINGS

Heskett, J., "Lessons in the Service Sector," *Harvard Business Review* (March-April 1987).

Holtz, H., *How to Succeed as an Independent Consultant* (New York: Wiley, 1983).

Kahn, J. P., "A Good Word about Consultants," *Inc.* (Jan. 1984).

Leavitt, H. J., *Managerial Psychology* (Chicago: University of Chicago Press, 1978).

Lippitt, G. L., *Helping across Cultures* (Washington, D. C.: International Consultants Foundation, 1978).

Lippitt, G. L. et al, *Implementing Organizational Change* (San Francisco: Jossey-Bass, 1985).

"Long-Distance Learning Gets an 'A' at Last," *Business Week* (May 9, 1988).

Moore, G. L., *The Politics of Management Consulting* (New York: Praeger, 1984).

Schein, E.H., *Process Consultation: Its Role in Organizational Development* (Reading, Mass.: Addison-Wesley, 1969).

Sloane, C. S., "The Road Ahead for Consulting," *Journal of Management Consulting* 3 (1) (1986).

Steele, F., *The Role of the Internal Consultant* (Boston: CBI Publishing, 1982).

Tierno, D. A., "Growth Strategies for Consulting in the Next Decade," *Sloan Management Review* (Winter 1986).

Woolsey, G., "On the Proper Training of Future Management," *Interfaces* 11 (4) (Aug. 1981).

CHAPTER 4

THE
NEW
MARKETING

TOUGHER CLIENTS, TOUGHER SALES

Given the new sophistication of clients, the unfortunate experience of some at the hands of charlatans and "pop management" hucksters, and the enormous increase in the number of consultants, it is no wonder that marketing consulting services has become a very challenging task. Where *Fortune* 1,000 companies formerly would award a major contract to a "name" consulting firm without much deliberation, today they require competitive bids from as many as a half-dozen firms. And where consultants formerly could assure themselves of a contract based solely on their own (or their partners') reputations, today they are asked to perform preliminary studies, often for no fees or merely for costs, prior to the submission of a major proposal. Nowadays, most clients need to be reassured that the consulting firm does, in fact, understand their industry and its unique problems, opportunities, and threats.

A second marketing challenge facing consultants these days stems from the same specialization we have already discussed. Even clients who used consultants only seldom in the past are now discovering the great variety of specialists available to assist them. In previous years, one consultant might build a relationship with one client that would result in a variety of different, specific jobs later—the classic "follow-on sale." Today, however, many clients will consider planning specialists only for planning projects, marketing specialists only for marketing projects, and so forth, particularly if no ongoing relationship has been developed.

Getting Quoted

"Does anything traditional still work?" one might ask. The answer, of course, is yes. A timeless approach, the cold-call letter, continues to be effective if used properly. It helped me get started almost twenty years ago; it is helping beginning consultants today and will probably be generating business for new independents twenty years from now.

A second classic and very powerful approach is to get on the speakers' circuit. I am constantly amazed at how few experienced consultants, mature business people with a gift for gab, know how to get invited to speak at major industry functions. It's really quite straightforward. You simply need to look for advance notice of conferences that are being held—in the various industry publications such as *Advertising Age* or *The American Banker* or in your local newspapers. The secret is in understanding that, for such industry bashes, a date must be picked well enough in advance that hotel accommodations can be guaranteed in the city selected. As a result, major conference organizers lock in the hotel first, and then announce, often six months to a year in advance, that the conference will be held. At this stage, a theme probably hasn't been selected yet, only the site and a block of hotel rooms. It is not too difficult, then, to contact the conference sponsors while everything is still in the planning stage and volunteer your services. Obviously, you will have to convince them that you know something about their industry or the topics to be covered; but I know from my own experience that most organizers are delighted to find new speakers for their conferences. Invariably they have been using the same ones for years and everyone in that industry is getting tired of hearing them.

■**CASE IN POINT**
In 1980 I read of a Bank Administration Institute conference to be held in three months in Miami on a topic on
which I had recently completed some research. I called BAI
in Chicago, offered my services, sent them an outline of
what I would talk about, and ended up on the BAI conference circuit for the next three years, speaking or directing
major workshops at more than a dozen national conferences on a variety of bank management issues.

GETTING PUBLISHED

63

A third traditional approach to business development that works
well is closely allied with one's success on the speakers' circuit:
getting your speeches published in industry trade journals.
Again, I never cease to be amazed at the number of veteran
consultants who approach me about how to get something published. It really is not difficult if you take the time and already
have some good raw material to work with, such as your most
recent speech to that industry. It is even easier if the speech is
still in your desktop computer memory and can be easily mas-
saged prior to a new printout. In other words, don't ever throw
anything away!

It is not hard to turn a speech into a smoothly worded article.
Each industry has its own trade publications. Banking, for example, has a daily newspaper, a weekly newspaper, several
monthly journals, and at least a half dozen quarterly journals,
and that's just in this country! If all the banking-related English
language publications directed out of London are included, the
number of publishing possibilities more than doubles. The same

holds true in engineering, hotel or hospital administration, metallurgy, and every other major business field. Then there are the various management disciplines and their professional affiliations and publications. For example, my field of study is business policy (strategic planning). Strategists have the Planning Forum out of Oxford, Ohio, an international network of strategic and corporate planners. It supports two strategy journals. There is also the *Journal of Business Strategy*. Finally, there are the academic "big time" publications such as the *Sloan Management Review*, the *Harvard Business Review*, the *California Management Review*, and a number of others, all of which encourage articulate business people to submit pragmatic pieces on current topics. You can even gain some exposure for yourself and practice your writing skills by submitting an opinion piece or a letter to the editor of your local newspaper. Such short pieces, directed at business problems and industry-related issues, have generated a good deal of business for my practice over the years.

There is no excuse for not being published if you have something important to say.

Remember, however, that in addition to having something to say, you also need to know how to write creatively. Many consultants were originally trained to write mechanistic, "canned" reports where not much more than the client's name changed from project to project. Some writers, raised on this kind of mechanistic management and consulting, find themselves unable to generate the fresh and creative new ideas that are called for when writing for the business journals or editorial columns. In a sense, it goes back to a basic question about management itself. In the 1960s and 1970s, it was usually argued that management was a science, a perspective that goes hand in hand with mechanistic values and approaches. But in the 1980s, many have recognized that management is an art—which implies that we need to be artistic and creative when dealing with or writing about the new organic processes of rebirth and renewal.

Through networking with industry trade groups and receiving exposure through speeches and articles, you can achieve a reputation as one of the industry's gurus. That, in turn, can help you to become a source of expert analysis for the local or even national press. It really doesn't hurt your consulting practice to have the *Los Angeles Times*, the *Wall Street Journal*, or a local television reporter call you for an opinion and quote you in print or on the air the next day.

65

TAKING OFF THE GLOVES

It used to be the major firms that relied on these kinds of indirect marketing approaches. But as consulting becomes more and more specialized and more and more experts emerge, the smaller, independent firms are profiting from industry-based speeches, articles, and other forms of indirect marketing. And among the major firms, truly titanic competitive battles are now starting to build. In fact, these heretofore gentlemanly competitors are resorting to the kind of primal direct marketing once reserved for smaller firms and independents—aggressive sales calls, pounding the concrete, and knocking on doors! In fact, the industry has done a complete flip in the last few years to the point where everyone is using every competitive tool available to generate billings.

■**CASE IN POINT**

The British advertising agency, Saatchi & Saatchi, which began acquiring U.S.-based consulting firms in 1984, is amassing a broad base of diverse firms with excellent reputations to achieve economies of scale with major clients and thus gain market share through classic price competition. Further, Saatchi & Saatchi believes that many of the large consulting practices have been run inefficiently, more as private clubs for the partners than as true service businesses in highly competitive markets. Following their acquisition of Hay & Associates, Saatchi & Saatchi executives implemented a policy whereby every consultant at Hay has some responsibility for business development and all managers and executives must generate prescribed levels of new volume annually or be asked to leave the firm. Such pressure to produce or "get out" has drastically altered the culture of the firm and driven a number of Hay old hands to seek work elsewhere or start their own practices. Those who have stayed are generally younger and more willing to put in the sixty-hour weeks such intensity requires. On the other hand, Hay & Associates has expanded its services well beyond its former compensation specialization into strategic planning and other disciplines, and the firm is now reported to be much more profitable than ever before.

66

The Big-8 accounting firms also are facing a renaissance as a result of aggressive new marketing practices. At such firms, locally based consultants report to a partner in charge (PIC— pronounced "pick") or practice unit head (PUH—pronounced "pooh") at each local office. For example, the management services group in the Dallas office would traditionally report to the PIC of the Dallas office, who is responsible not only for management services but also audit and tax services. He is measured on how well his geographic area performs. He has, as a rule, no motivation to assist anyone outside his geographic area and will do so only when he has idle staff. This traditional territorial orientation tended to prevent the Big-8 from developing truly competitive services much beyond accounting and DP systems because it was only in these limited areas that every office had relatively equal talent. Major offices such as New York, Chicago, or San Francisco would develop consulting capabilities beyond these disciplines, often specialized to serve a particular industry prominent in that geographical area, but they would be limited to the practice of that office—first, because the PIC wanted to be sure he got credit for whatever was done; and second, because if these specialist consultants were off helping some other office, they couldn't be at home, helping to expand existing client relationships. It was all very petty and medieval. It also cost the Big-8 billions in consulting fees over the period 1965-85 because whenever someone contacted a Big-8 firm wanting generalist or specialist consulting support in Austin or Oklahoma City or Omaha or Sacramento, they were assured that "the local office can handle it," when in fact the only thing the local office had to offer was an audit staff with limited consulting experience. After a while, executives just stopped calling on the Big-8 accounting firms for help beyond accounting or DP systems. The other 90 percent of the consulting market moved to full-time consulting practices.

Several things have come to pass, however, that have strained the archaic Big-8 territorial issues to their limits. First, in the early 1980s, the whole accounting field began open competition for qualified staff—advertising, recruiting each other's people, and so forth. Second, in spite of the geographic limitations, many of the partnerships found their management services billings equal to or exceeding their audit revenues. In order to sustain growth, the audit-based partners had to begin listening to the consulting-based partners, and they began demanding market and management changes more in line with consulting practices rather than traditional audit practices. Third, as we have already discussed, a number of clients began demanding specialized industry knowledge and expertise as prerequisites to even the simplest of consulting relationships.

In the ensuing years, Ernst & Whinney, like Arthur Andersen, has evolved away from the audit side of its practices and developed a national preeminence in health care and financial services consulting, while Peat Marwick Main has developed specialties in manufacturing automation and robotics and strategic services. In turn, these efforts explain why some Big-8 firms have rocketed into the upper ranks of all consulting organizations with respect to total billings. Those accounting firms still unable to break with the old, territorial paradigm have at least developed SWAT teams to address the national needs of one particular industry or another, even where audit partners still dominate the partnership.

The same demand for specialized industry knowledge has forced many of the majors to reassess their business development efforts. Industry giants that prided themselves on their generalist approach to any and all problems have been driven by market and competitive forces to adopt industry expertise and specialization, too. The larger regional consulting firms have not stood still, either. Many of the more successful ones have developed new business from discrete, self-funded industry research projects, the results of which are released at public conferences where dozens of potential client firms are invited to hear the results. Some of the more popular topics range from international marketing and export sales to doing business with the People's Republic of China.

The independent networks, watching the larger, regional, and national firms put on expensive conferences and R&D sessions, also have started to develop alliances with local business people

68

and hold workshops for small businesses. In the Los Angeles area, for example, I am aware of several groups comprised of local lawyers, independent CPAs, investment advisors, and management consultants that have pooled their resources and invited managers and owners of small companies in the area to day-long seminars with broad-based agendas combining sessions on business planning methodology with reviews of the new tax laws and investment strategies for raising additional capital.

Even the academic independents have their own approach for generating new business. Working with smaller, new enterprises, some academic consultants will accept lower fees in exchange for the right to publish research articles or use the firm as a source of projects for graduate students. Others generate business for themselves by waiving fees in exchange for early stock options and a seat on the board. The late Professor Doriot of Harvard had such an arrangement early on with DEC. When he died in 1987, his estate held more than $52 million of DEC stock.

69

GETTING A COMPUTER

One of the emerging trends from all this competition is more artistic visual and oral presentations—what used to be called slide shows. The bad news is that it is becoming increasingly difficult these days to maintain a successful practice, even an independent one, without the aid of a powerful desk-top computer, like a new-generation IBM or a Macintosh Plus. The good news is that these management tools provide even the smallest practice with the capability of generating art work that formerly required professional artists and a great deal of money. Some of the desk-top publishing programs coupled with laser and five-color printers can generate pages of professionally created art work, pie charts, graphs, or simply summaries of verbal presentations. These are printed out and duplicated on clear or colored plastic overlays on any state-of-the-art copier, and the result is a $5,000 presentation for a few hours' work and $15 worth of supplies.

The use of computers and sophisticated programming doesn't start and stop with art work when it comes to business development. Traditionally, consultants would ask a prospect for their last few years' annual reports and then perform manual or calculator-based analyses of the financials in a search for issues, ills, or points of discussion. Often it would take half a day to review thoroughly the financials of a complex company. Today, desk-top computers and the analytical software that supports them can generate far more detailed and sophisticated analyses in just a few minutes.

THE STATE OF THE ART

Here again, just as clients have become more sophisticated, so too have consultant marketing efforts. The marketing methods that were formerly the preserve of the largest, most sophisticated firms are available now to any independent who specializes enough to target a speech or an article to a specific audience. Conversely, the mass marketing techniques like cold-calls and letter campaigns, once looked down on by the prestigious firms, now are used by them to comb every last viable prospect out of the marketplace. Independents have sophisticated computer graphics and analytical programs at their fingertips that give them the opportunity to present themselves and their firms as highly mature, technically sophisticated practices. With a number of independents forming allegiances within which to market locally, regional firms investing major amounts in focused research for business development purposes, and the largest firms struggling to remake themselves according to the new paradigm of specialization, consultant marketing has become as sophisticated, if not more so, in this industry as in any other profession today. The traditionalist approaches based on leasing posh offices downtown or being a member at the local country club just don't generate any credibility in light of the new competition and increased client skepticism.

We're ready, again, to summarize how the new management paradigm affects what clients are looking for and how consultants are marketing themselves:

71

Mechanistic Management	Organic Management
Clients:	
Sought "name" firms	Seek consultants with appropriate specialist knowledge
Awarded contracts casually	Demand competitive bids
Add-on business the norm	Add-on business goes to the most qualified
Assumed consultant expertise	Demand proof of expertise
Bought external help readily	Cost justify every contract
Consultants:	
Often sold extemporaneously	Develop complex, computer-based presentations
Large firms sold indirectly	Independents sell indirectly through focus
Small firms cold-call	Large firms cold-call and canvas, too
Once established, sold indirectly	Every major sale now a direct, planned effort

Mechanistic Management Consultants:	Organic Management
Sold off generalist approach	Sell off specialist and industry expertise
Used location and affiliations	Use public conferences and research forums
Sold off extant reputation	Work continually at strengthening reputation
Printed slick brochures	Marketing augmented with industry speeches and op-ed page articles

For consultants, this developing paradigm now means no quarter given, no "gimmies" in the marketplace, even among your oldest and best clients, and an ever-increasing level of competition. Those who wish to survive must maintain constant state-of-the-art postures with the industries they serve and the disciplines they practice.

RECOMMENDED READINGS

Bermont, H., *Psychological Strategies for Success in Consulting* (Washington, D.C.: The Consultants Library, 1983.

Block, P., *Flawless Consulting: A Guide to Getting Your Expertise Used* (Austin, Tex.: Learning Concepts, 1981).

Cohen, W. A., *How to Make It Big as a Consultant* (New York: AMACOM, 1985).

Connor, R. A. and J. P. Davidson, *Marketing Your Consulting and Professional Services* (New York: Wiley, 1985).

Gowan, V. Q., *Consulting to Government* (Cambridge, Mass.: Infoscan, 1979).

Holtz, H., *The Consultant's Edge: Using the Computer as a Marketing Tool* (New York: Wiley, 1985).

Kadushin, A., *Consultation in Social Work* (New York: Columbia University Press, 1977).

Kennedy, James H., ed., "Public Relations for Management Consultants: A Practical Compendium," *Consultants News* (1980).

————"The 25 'Best' Proposals by Management Consulting Firms," *Consultants News* (1984).

Kotler, P. and P. N. Bloom, *Marketing Professional Services* (Englewood Cliffs, N. J.: Prentice-Hall, 1984).

Wilson, A., *Practice Development for Professional Firms* (London: McGraw-Hill, 1984).

Zinsser, W. K., *On Writing Well* (New York: Harper & Row, 1976).

CHAPTER 5

NEW STRATEGIC SERVICES

The whole idea of strategic planning has changed so quickly over the past few years that consultants have been hard pressed to keep up. There has been, correspondingly, a severe loss in clients' confidence. Firms that previously specialized in this field are struggling to find new values and new ways to assist their clients. But strategic planning remains a tough sell these days, especially when dealing with sophisticated clients or those facing decline.

OLD MODELS, NEW PARADIGMS

Fifteen or twenty years ago, surprisingly few *Fortune* 500 firms performed effective strategic planning. In the late 1960s, George Steiner sent a survey to the CEOs of the *Fortune* 500 asking about their jobs and roles in their respective companies. In response, some 350 agreed that strategic planning was one of their most critical responsibilities, yet less than one-third indicated that they spent more than 15 percent of their time actually making plans or formulating strategy. I believe that the major reason managers neglected strategic planning then is that they focused on operations and operational planning. In the mid-1980s, a survey by Ben Tregoe, of the firm of Kepner-Tregoe (which gave us the classic strategic concept of the nine Driving Forces), indicated that managers still preferred to focus on short-term profit goals instead of long-term strategy. Too many American managers still just don't know how to think in terms of broad strategic issues and plans.

The strategic planning done by some of the largest firms in the late 1960s was essentially a process of extrapolating from the present situation. Consultants became the magi of the discipline—wise men bearing gifts in the form of planning models like the Boston Consulting Group's 4-box Product Matrix and Experience Curve Model or the Harvard Business School's concept of distinctive competence. Today, such models are passé, but they were considered revolutionary twenty or even ten years ago. These mechanistic models helped the Housekeepers control their enormous organizations while providing the illusion of a more creative approach to product lines and markets. Many consultants thought they would be working with these models forever—or at least until retirement.

In the 1970s, however, things started moving too quickly for the old models to be useful. First, as we have seen throughout this book, there was a growing awareness that global markets and global competition were drastically and permanently changing the needs of American business. Simultaneously, people realized that some companies were just better managed and more efficient than others. These organic, market-driven organizations, with a fanatical dedication to their customers, their workers, and the quality of their products, had six to ten times the productivity of other companies, and all the planning models in the world had nothing to do with it. The firms that were winning out, in the face of severe new competition, didn't seem to be doing it with the help of classic strategic models. In a few short years, consultants and clients committed to those old models were both becoming obsolete.

At the same time, as we have also seen throughout, some companies and industries had passed the mature part of their respective business cycles and were entering a stage of real decline. The strategy models became even less relevant for companies struggling with the fundamental problem of survival. An industry in decline can be described as one in which

- Volume is ebbing,
- Margins are shrinking,
- Technology is not proprietary,
- There is little product differentiation,
- Price is the key to sales,
- Overcapacity is rampant.

So that here, again, the classic models of strategic planning don't seem to be working for companies facing these drastic, immediate threats to their existence.

Action and reaction

Given these issues, most senior executives felt that long-range planning was a futile exercise. A number of large corporations gave up strategic planning altogether or shut down their internal planning departments, believing the best they could do was *react* to the external threats coming at them faster and faster. They also turned to process consultants and asked, "Help us become *proactive* and regain control." But there is a certain false logic in assuming that the reactive or proactive approaches are mutually exclusive, and such managers were failing to understand that an effective strategy now required two different forms of planning. As Toffler explains, the traditional, reactive approach develops strategic plans in the light of *probable* scenarios of future events, but these scenarios seldom take all possible contingencies into account in an environment where technologies and markets are changing at lightning speed and where the old planning models lose their usefulness. Proactive planning, on the other hand, seeks to identify the *least probable* future possibilities with the highest potential impact. Today's consultants must deliver a mix of this proactive planning for the most uncertain kinds of contingencies and more traditional, reactive strategy in which the consultant asks all the right "What if?" and "Why not?" questions.

■ **Case in point**
Professor Ian Mitroff heads the Center for Crisis Management at USC. Through the center, he works with *Fortune* 500 enterprises to develop organic approaches to contin-

gency planning for worst-case scenarios—Bhopal, Chernoble, product tampering, and so forth. He stresses, however, that this capability must be added to the existing strategic efforts of visionary CEOs rather than become a single, predominant planning focus.

The old models also failed us in the area of vertical and horizontal diversification. Instead of developing global organizations able to compete effectively in dozens of markets, most American conglomerates of the 1960s and 1970s became just bloated, inept, and inefficient. Many of these megacorporations used—or misused—the familiar strategic planning models. But all those models seemed to do for the senior managers of these companies was teach them to use mergers to amass, rather than create, value; and those managers went on to treat their shareholders as though they were second-class citizens. Their acquisitions generally were not backed up by real strategic analysis and were thus incapable of helping the company meet its long-range goals and objectives, if indeed they had any.

American managers need to learn the same lessons whenever they lose the protection of regulated industries or begin exporting their products in a free-wheeling trade environment. Fortunately, there are some innovative new approaches to strategy now emerging. I'd like to look at the ideas of three individuals—one a consultant, one an educator, and one an executive—who, taking separate paths, have each developed strategic approaches for a new business environment during a period when most traditional planning consultants have fallen out of favor.

THE EXPONENTIAL CURVE OF CHANGE

The first strategy sage of the mid- to late 1980s is Mike Naylor, who is, of all things, senior vice president for strategic planning at General Motors. Although GM itself may not be responding very well to change, Naylor's thinking is quite prescient. He observes, first, that humans have been on Earth for about 800 life times (LTs); lived in constructed housing about 150 LTs; measured time for about 80 LTs; used modern communications for approximately 4 LTs; used electric motors for 2 LTs; and used most familiar consumer goods, from teflon pots to nylon socks, from Macintosh computers to plastic disposable razors, from VCRs, to digital laser discs, only in this most recent 1 LT. In other words, the very rate of change is increasing faster and faster, in relentless, exponential fashion. Naylor points out that this exponential curve of development and change faces us in every market in which we deal. In essence, Naylor is warning us that the very conditions of reality have changed.

Like it or not, change is the one constant of the universe—and it is coming at us ever faster and in ever-greater magnitudes.

This exponential curve of change, Naylor advises, may be reaching the point where CEOs of mature organizations can no longer handle it. For example, the average tenure of such an individual in a *Fortune* 500 company is about seven years. In that time, a CEO may go to his board once and ask for, say, $500 million to remodel a plant. In so doing, he hopes he will be leaving a permanent mark on the firm, and the implementation of that one project or megachange might well consume the remainder of his active career. But with the change curve becoming ever tighter, Naylor asks, "What if our CEO has to go to his board twice in his tenure or once every two years, for another $500 million, just to keep pace with the business environment? Will he be able to handle it? Will the board tolerate it? Can the company itself absorb such rates of change?"

Given that change is now the norm, management policy can no longer focus on stability. Most managers seem to think that *management* means maintaining the status quo and resisting change, a kind of false logic that probably comes from classic models of finance and accounting and the idea that once a budget and annual profit plan are developed, management must spend all of its energies identifying and reducing variances from the plan. After six, eight, or ten years in the trenches dealing with such demands, is it any wonder that successful managers have trouble understanding that change should be accepted and exploited for competitive advantage? Senior managers have gotten where they are by their success at suppressing change only to be promoted to positions responsible for, in effect, creating and channeling change. "Things," as Alice said in Wonderland, "are getting curiouser and curiouser!"

The lesson for strategy consultants in all this is that first, they must devote a good deal of their time to understanding the concept of unrelenting, exponential change; second, they must study how the industries they serve have been changing; and third, they must find a resource to help them improve their process consulting skills. This change curve is so potentially threatening to managers used to maintaining the status quo that it simply cannot be shared with clients in the aggressive, prescriptive manner of traditional content consulting. Even the most receptive of clients will stop listening, and the relationship will be lost. Rather, what must take place is a series of nonthreatening discussions about the undeniable changes that are altering the industry and the company in which you help your client reach the acceptance stage as soon as possible. I like to use a series of related questions:

- How did you make money five years ago?
- How are you making it now?
- How might you be making it five years from now?

Or:

- Who were your customers five or ten years ago?
- Who are they now?
- Who might they be five years from now?

Or:

- What products did you rely on five or ten years ago?
- Which ones do you rely on now?
- Which ones might become obsolete in the next five years?
- Which new products might have to be developed within another five years?

By drawing clients into a discussion of how things have already changed, an effective process consultant can move them toward acceptance and help them to begin thinking about how things will continue to change, eventually bringing the discussion around to managing change and finally managing change as a normal part of their business, not as an aberration.

BECOMING THE 800-POUND GORILLA

Kenichi Ohmae is director of McKinsey & Company's Tokyo office. Among his many credentials, he holds a Ph.D. in nuclear engineering from MIT. Since 1978 he has written eight books on strategy. The first one to be translated into English was *The Mind of the Strategist* in 1982, followed shortly thereafter by *Triad Power*. Ohmae's approach in counseling American and Japanese managers has been to analyze the successful strategies of Japanese manufacturers who have become what I call "800-pound gorillas" who, as in the old joke, can do whatever they want in their respective marketplaces. Ohmae does not dwell on which country has more productive workers or stronger social values, nor does he talk about long-range planning models. Instead, he concentrates on basic strategic maneuvers in the here and now, and the ability to create product life cycles too short for competitors to compete against—as a company like Casio has done by developing and marketing new calculator models faster than anyone else. Ohmae has taught American managers a fundamental lesson about the interrelatedness of market share and strategy.

Whoever has the largest share of the market controls your company because they set the standards of price, quality, and perceived customer value, and so are making your decisions for you.

To defend oneself in such an environment, Ohmae suggests that managers develop a three-pronged strategy built on competitor-based, customer-based and corporate-based ideologies. The role of strategy is to help managers find ways to reduce costs, lower prices, and increase volume, a slice at a time, a fraction of market share at a time, until local gains become regional successes, and regional successes become worldwide acceptance. Such "win the world" tactics, in other words, help 150-pound gorillas eventually become 800-pound gorillas.

Consultants working in this discipline, then, must learn a great deal about cost management and its precise application to their client's industry. The elements of cost management in hospital administration, for example, are quite different than they are in the airline or telecommunications industries. Fast-food firms have different cost management and pricing issues than do industrial enterprises. In fact, as Ohmae teaches us, it is impossible to reduce costs without a detailed, technical knowledge of the business; and it is impossible, in turn, to maximize market share without the achievement of the lowest possible costs. This is one more reason that the old generalist consulting paradigm doesn't work anymore.

DEVELOPING COMPETITIVE ADVANTAGE

Mike Porter of the Harvard Business School has written a few books, too. He first published *Competitive Strategy* and then, more recently, *Competitive Advantage.* His approach resembles Ohmae's in its emphasis on the market and the customer. But Porter breaks down market issues into a matrix of inbound logistics, operations, outbound logistics, marketing and sales, and service on the horizontal axis with firm infrastructure, human resource management, technological development, and procurement on the vertical axis, which he calls his "value chain." The model is an elaborate checklist for managers to test themselves and their organizations at every step and in every area as to whether costs and prices are minimized and volume and productivity maximized.

We have already glanced at Porter's second major concept— that there are only two ways to gain market share. Either a company maximizes cost control and has the lowest price in the market, capturing market share through head-on price competition, or it develops something called value added—a perception on the part of customers that the firm's products or services are of the highest quality and worth paying for. Porter, too, has taught American business an essential lesson.

Go high or go low, but for God's sake, don't get stuck in the middle. That's where most companies (and guaranteed failure) can be found.

Obviously, there is a great deal more in Mike Porter's books. The essential point to be stressed here, however, is that managers must deliver quality at competitive prices based on cost management and productivity. Consultants, accordingly, must help clients look at and break down their markets and their organizations in new and different ways. We must ask our clients and ourselves

- Who are the purveyors of value added?
- How vulnerable are they and why?
- Who are the low-cost providers?
- How much lower are their prices and why?
- What can our client do to further reduce costs and undercut those prices?

- How can the firm take a cost-management approach to the principal functions of the organization?
- How can we, as consultants, "make things happen" with this client's organization?

The essential cost-cutting strategies can be delivered either in a process or content mode depending on the receptiveness and needs of the client.

A further area for consultants specializing in strategic services as a part of this new consulting paradigm is the concept of productivity. Consultants can play a valuable role by trying to answer some of the following questions:

- What is productivity and how should it be measured?
- What constitutes productive work within the organization?
- Is it the same thing from company to company or even in different areas of the same company?
- How much input should employees have in defining and establishing the criteria for productivity?
- What are the best methods to implement Quality Circles and other productivity-improvement techniques?

As Bob Sabath, Vice President with A. T. Kearney (and 1988 IMC President) relates, "The role of the process consultant is to incubate effectiveness first (doing the right things) before helping to improve efficiency (doing things right)."

I will discuss some of these issues more fully in Chapters 8 and 9, but I raise them here to emphasize the integral part productivity plays today in reducing costs, lowering price, and gaining market share.

CLIENT STRATEGIC NEEDS

Consultants who continue to market strategic assistance in the form of analytical tools to evaluate experience curves, or who help clients find new markets only through acquisitions, or who attempt to reduce costs without showing how such cost reduction can be passed on to customers are already obsolete. Bob Atteyah, a director of the Los Angeles office of McKinsey & Co., and someone who has devoted his career to strategy development across a number of industries, states that he has not seen one of the old planning matrices in years. Clients are looking for organic ways to change the culture of their firms from internally combative to holistic, from political to caring, from products offered to market needs driven. These same clients are interested not in hot tub management and all its gimmicks, but in real approaches to quality of work life and its successful management; not in esoteric computer models or charts demonstrating financial history, but practical, shirt-sleeves approaches to productivity improvement and cost reduction. For clients who find themselves in mature industries, this means

- Gearing the organization around markets and profit centers,
- Insisting on the real facts,
- Understanding the economics of the firm's profits,

- Knowing where all the costs are, fixed and variable, and making certain all the managers do also,
- Creating a detailed segmentation of the market,
- Reorganizing the marketing effort around growth markets,
- Maintaining a lean staff,
- Continually reassessing and adjusting strategy,

Clients also need to recognize that such conversions are expensive because the time and energy that go into dealing with such changes will be lost from what is currently considered "productive work." Many a management team has articulated its commitment to new management values only to shy away from them quickly when they came to understand how much effort and expense would be required. Even CEOs desperate for change are sometimes not willing to pay for the recklessness of previous decades or the havoc loosed on profits by deregulation.

Helping clients deal emotionally and practically with the enormous costs of managing and implementing change is perhaps the most difficult aspect of strategy consulting these days. According to Ben Tregoe, whose survey of American managers' strategic values we looked at in the beginning of this chapter, "American managers are very strong in operations management, but have done a terrible job of developing strategic disciplines." Tregoe goes on to draw an engaging pictogram as shown on page 87. On the horizontal axis is strategic competence (the *what*) and on the vertical axis, operations competence (the *how*). The pluses and minuses denote strength or weakness in each particular area. Therefore, a firm that was strong operationally but weak strategically would fall into quadrant 2. A firm weak in both strategy and operations would be found in quadrant 4.

Such managers, Tregoe informs us, perceive themselves in a pit of alligators, and it is useless talking strategy to them as long as they feel their lives are threatened. The pressure on CEOs for short-term earnings plays havoc on any efforts to develop the

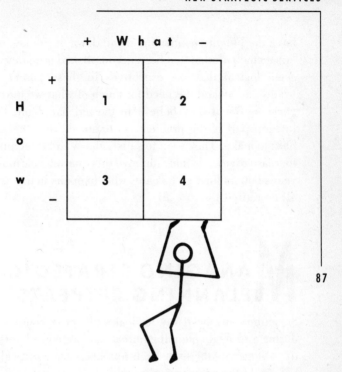

longer-range strategies that can slowly but surely win market share. Some zealously adopt the principles of cost management merely to improve short-term bottom-line results a little bit rather than reduce prices now so as to increase volume and market share later. This is particularly true when dealing with the subsidiary of some giant holding company or conglomerate. Several times in the past few years, I have worked very hard with the CEO of a major enterprise to develop new strategies, new corporate values, and new organizational structures, only to have the parent organization come down at the last minute and erase much of what had been accomplished or planned. It would seem logical that the executives in these parent companies would understand the need for much of what we have been discussing. But if they believe in the old paradigm, they are an integral part of the problem, so to speak, and the sale will be hard to make. They want to satisfy the Wall Street analysts *now;* increase dividends *now;* improve this quarter's earnings and this year's bottom line. (Who cares what happens in five years? We'll all be retired!)

Managing Strategic Planning Retreats

Sometimes the best way to deal with these complex issues is during a strategic planning retreat, and for consultants, the ability to stage and facilitate such retreats is more critical than ever before. In the past, typically, the top six or eight officers of the corporation would take two to three days and go away to discuss business plans and major problems. All too often, however, these retreats would become merely platforms for the CEO's pet projects or excuses for the top executives to raise a little hell at a nice resort several times a year. In other firms, more and more managers were invited so that the retreats became less decision-making sessions and more just a way to reward or recognize hard-working managers throughout the organization. None of this is wrong or bad. Every organization under stress needs to develop a mechanism to reward and recognize its best managers, allow its top executives to unwind, and permit them an occasional primal scream. But the firm still must address strategic issues that cannot be dealt with during the frenzy and pressures of everyday operations. A strategic retreat provides the time and energy necessary for managers to discuss, define, formalize, and analyze issues such as:

- A clear definition of their business,
- Minimum acceptable returns for shareholders,
- Dividend and reinvestment policies,
- Where they are in the life cycle of their industry and their organization,
- The type of management required to manage that life cycle stage,
- Policies of research and development,
- Management values regarding customer service, product quality, and markets to be served,
- The rate of growth to be pursued,
- Standards of measurement to evaluate progress,
- The kind of people to be hired,
- The investment to be made in staff development,
- Relationships between the firm and its community.

These and many other crucial issues and business policies can be developed only after in-depth discussion and study. Accordingly, I now advise clients that trying to review all these issues in a single, two- or three-day retreat is sheer folly. I advise them to select four or five issues to be dealt with in-depth until clear policy statements can be developed around the decisions made. A major part of my job is also providing some research on the issues as they pertain to the client's industry. This includes digging up articles and developing meaningful questions that then are delivered several weeks in advance of the retreat so that the participants can better prepare themselves for the discussions.

At such working retreats, no more than ten executives are allowed to facilitate decision making, extracurricular activities are kept to a minimum, and no alcohol flows before the evening session is completed, often as late as 10 P.M. Every three to four months, similar retreats are held until all of the firm's strategic issues are resolved. But strategy is, as Mike Naylor suggests, a management tool to deal with a constantly changing world. Therefore, having spent the better part of two years reviewing and updating major policies and strategy, it usually is time to begin the cycle all over again, starting with basic assumptions about the business.

However, the planning doesn't stop at the retreat. Henry Mintzberg at McGill University, who has amassed sixteen years of research about strategic management and planning, argues that strategies are not always deliberate but can emerge over time as companies experiment and respond to competition. Further, there is no single right way to plan or develop strategy. Effective plans arise out of experimentation as well as systematic planning methodologies or a combination of both. There is a fluidity to strategy development, and planning, if it is to be successful in the long term, should take place at different levels on different horizons using different tools throughout the organization. This requires the strategy consultant to assure that planning is performed effectively by more than just senior management. The planning process must include training programs for managers and perhaps individual department planning sessions.

BACK TO THE BASICS

Not too long ago, Adrian Payne, a professor of management at the University of Melbourne in Australia, wrote an article summarizing his extensive research on various worldwide management consulting firms specializing in strategic services. Payne argued, and I strongly agree, that some client firms are returning to basic management and strategy techniques—partly because global competition has forced them into straightforward cost management, and partly because they now recognize the folly of relying too heavily on strategic models, such as the portfolio model, that have caused numerous companies to lose their momentum and creativity. Some client firms have been pulling their strategic efforts inside themselves, forgoing the use of external strategy consultants in lieu of bright M.B.A.s on corporate staff. There have been some terrific examples of this kind of return to basics! Gulf & Western, for example, sold off fifty companies, thus raising $700 million for redeployment and renewal. The companies they sought to acquire with this new cash were subject to a simple yet rigorous criteria. They

- Must not be in capital-intensive industries,
- Must not be inordinately affected by foreign competition,
- Must be in a predominantly service business,
- Must have high operating margins and no leveraging.

91

Over a five-year period these efforts produced both a nose dive in gross revenues and an enormous improvement in earnings, and the Gulf & Western share price climbed from $18 to $78. At American Can Company, similarly, between 1977 and 1986, management scrapped its old strategies and literally sold off everything the company held, so that by 1986 the firm did not own a single business it had held a decade earlier. American Can, previously a dowdy packaging company deep in a stage of decline, transited through thirty divestitures and fifteen acquisitions to a financial services and retailing enterprise with a P/E ratio of 16 to 1.

THE RED QUEEN SYNDROME AND THE INEVITABILITY OF CHANGE

Other companies—especially those who historically embraced strategic models and continue to have a strong urge to be first in their industry to use the very latest strategic thinking—are heating up the strategic consulting arena by dropping old consulting firms in favor of new ones offering organic planning methods. Even one of the great model makers himself, Bruce Henderson, chairman of The Boston Consulting Group, admits that most of the familiar BCG models are now passé. In their place have emerged concepts of Bourgeois Competition, Darwinian Fitness, and The Red Queen Syndrome. Although the first two are self-explanatory, the third may require some explanation. In *Alice in Wonderland*, Alice runs into the Red Queen who maintains her rule through unpredictability and an irascible personality, screaming, "Off with her head!" for wholly illogical reasons. There is a marketing strategy model that makes a good case for using such nonpredictability and bluff to keep one's opponents in the marketplace off balance. In any case, as Henderson concludes, "The key has shifted from having a strategy to being able to change a strategy."

The same point may apply to consulting firms as well as to business in general. Certainly strategic management services are leading the way for the dynamic growth and change of the entire consulting industry. There has always been strong competition between the major firms specializing in strategic management (BCG, Temple Barker & Sloane, Bain & Co., SPA and Braxton) and the major generalists that have a deep but not exclusive commitment to strategy (McKinsey & Co., Booz, Allen, ADL and A. T. Kearney). The competition will become even more heated into the twenty-first century, not only among these fierce competitors but between them as a bloc and many regional firms, now developing their own state-of-the-art strategic competence. Meanwhile, some companies are deciding to go it alone in their strategic deliberations, at least for the next few years, so as to reduce their reliance on outside gurus—except, perhaps, for the occasional process specialist who knows how to run a tight retreat and ask meaningful questions.

The implications should be clear for consultants who perceive themselves as specialists in strategy. Our prime responsibility must be to help clients realize the extent of the effort required to adopt the new paradigms of management and business. To do this we, in turn, must be knowledgeable in all the latest strategic approaches and models, be able to separate utility from fad, and provide meaningful counsel to our clients through a clear understanding of their needs.

RECOMMENDED READINGS

Abbegglen, J. C., and G. Stalk, Jr., *Kaisha, The Japanese Corporation* (New York: Basic Books, 1985).

Ansoff, H. I., "The Emerging Paradigm of Strategic Behavior," *Strategic Management Journal* 8 (6) (Nov.-Dec. 1987).

Bart, C. K. and R. E. White "Managing to Make Business Unit Strategies Work," *Planning Review* 14 (3) (May 1986).

Batts, W.L., "Dart and Kraft: From Merger to Strategic Management," *Planning Review* 13 (6) (November 1985).

Drake, R. L. "Innovative Structures for Managing Change," *Planning Review* 14 (6) (November 1986).

Dutton, J. E. and R. B. Dutton, "The Influence of the Strategic Planning Process on Strategic Change," *Strategic Management Journal* 8 (1987).

Goold, M., and A. Campbell, "Many Best Ways to Make Strategy," *Harvard Business Review* 65 (6) (Nov.-Dec. 1987).

Hammermesh, R. G., *Making Strategy Work: How Senior Managers Produce Results* (New York: Wiley, 1986).

Leontiades, M., *Managing The Unmanageable: Strategies for Success within the Conglomerate* (Reading, Mass.: Addison-Wesley, 1986).

Metzger, R. O. "Mental Gymnastics I, II, & III," *Bankers Monthly* (May, June, July 1986).

Metzger, R. O., I. I. Mitroff, and S. E. Rau, "Challenging the Strategic Assumptions of the Banking Industry," *Bankers Magazine*, 167 (4) (July-Aug. 1984).

Ohmae, K., *The Mind of the Strategist* (New York: McGraw-Hill, 1982).

Porter, M. E., *Competitive Strategy: Techniques for Analyzing Industries and Competitors* (New York: Free Press, 1980).

Rho, B.H., "A Comparison of Long Range Planning in South Korea, Japan and the U.S.," *Planning Review* 15 (2) (March-April 1987).

CHAPTER 6

NEW ORGANIZATION DESIGNS

THE GOOD OLD DAYS

When I first began consulting in the early 1970s, most large organizations needed help with mechanistic problems: either improving communications (the left hand didn't know what the right one was doing), or resolving conflict (the left hand was trying to cut off the right one). In the clarity of historical perspective, these fundamental problems arose because Housekeeper managers, trained and educated in the 1950s and 1960s, had only the barest inklings of the organic principles taught in the then new fields of Organization Development and Organizational Behavior. Many consultants weren't well versed in these new disciplines, either. But consultants did realize, at least, that organizations and their employees performed better when they had clear position (or job) descriptions, when committees were kept to the minimum through the effective delegation of authority and responsibility, and when organizational structure was as flat as possible. Fifteen or twenty years ago, a consultant could build a solid career, and do some companies a lot of good, by concentrating on these basic issues.

In those days, consulting often required the use of extensive employee questionnaires to identify common organizational problems—inappropriate reporting relationships, fuzzy lines of authority, or ineffective upward, downward, or lateral communications. Consultants devised complex questionnaires that helped to identify areas in the organization where employees were seeking change or where they were resisting change. The data from such surveys added credibility to consultants' recommendations and helped gain acceptance for those recommendations from employees whose concerns had been directly addressed. The final reports, embellished with dozens of detailed, mechanical position descriptions (PDs) and hand-drawn organization charts, would run from 150 to 300 pages, depending on the size of the organization under study. Given the state of the art, producing these organization audits was good but laborious work. Many such reports ended up serving as the equivalent of a policy manual, and I have clients today who still refer to them on points of corporate policy or philosophy. More often, however, those 300-page, comprehensively researched and elaborately designed reports ended up in someone's desk drawer or collecting dust on somebody's credenza.

PAST AND FUTURE

Clients today still need solid data bases of information and analyses of the root causes of organizational problems, but today's issues of rebirth and renewal demand new and different solutions and different types of reports. Consultants today are producing organic, creative, primarily *visual* reports that are intended to serve as tools of communication supported by discussion between consultant and client. The new consultants do not impose their values on client issues. They present the facts and ask clients, "What do you want to do now?" Often, clients will develop their own solutions from the consultant's "What if?" and "Why not?" questions, or work with their consultants in ongoing relationships to discover solutions.

Here again, this fluid, inward-directed style of problem solving is appropriate when dealing with today's increasingly sophisticated clients. Companies with more than 100 employees often now have bright HRM staff with M.B.A.s who are capable of performing their own creative renewal projects. Such managers, if they graduated in the last eight or ten years, have probably been exposed to more organization theory and case studies than consultants who began in the 1960s and 1970s. Other companies have hired "the best and the brightest" from firms such

96

as Hay & Associates or from leading business school faculties to direct their HRM and compensation-support functions. As a result, it is becoming more difficult each year to make the classic and formerly "easy" $50,000 to $250,000 sale of an organization audit.

The business environment of the 1980s and '90s, furthermore, demands more than just a new format for audits and consultant reports. Leading organizational theorists in the past decade have also shown that organizations themselves need new and different designs. No one disputes Larry Greiner's classic model of organizational evolution, which he published in the *Harvard Business Review* in 1972 under the title "Evolution and Revolution as Organizations Grow." Greiner showed that those *Fortune* 500 companies that had survived for at least fifty years (not many) evolved through five primary stages of growth interspersed by various crises anywhere from five to ten years apart. He demonstrated that such firms move from stages of entrepreneurship and creativity, to professional management and strong direction, to delegation and coordination of multiple divisions, and finally to collaboration around sophisticated, complex, and often multinational themes and issues. But in 1972 Greiner stopped his model at the collaboration stage, leaving the reader to speculate about the next possible evolutionary crisis. Today, the power of Greiner's idea lives on. In a recent article in the *California Management Review*, Tushman, Newman, and Romanelli note that almost all effective organizational evolution follows Greiner's model, which they call "convergence and upheaval." They reiterate that most organizations (and managers) muddle along until the muddling leads to crisis, when there must be a revolution in the management style, strategy, organization, and even the product line in order for the corporation to survive. This is another, more sophisticated version of the organizational life cycle of decline, denial, acceptance, and renewal.

For consultants, understanding where a company is along Greiner's evolutionary line and describing in some detail its current stage in the life cycle are tantamount to predicting its future. Through such understanding, consultants can help clients "see" into the future of their organizations and recognize common issues and problems before they arise. For the largest and oldest survivors on Greiner's original list of companies—some of which are so large and so geographically diffused that they cannot know or control all of their operating units well (and have thus been exposed to corporate raids on undervalued and practically forgotten assets)—I think the next crisis may be "Divestiture" followed by a five- to seven-year period of rebirth and renewal in which the needs of the market once again become the company's driving force.

98

WORK DESIGN

Under the relentless external pressure of global competition and corporate raiders, and the equally threatening internal pressure of new technologies and automation, corporate organization structures are changing rapidly and sometimes tumultuously. It has to be downright scary for a CEO, especially a Housekeeper, to witness all this change and realize that the young people in the organization have radically different viewpoints, expectations, and values. Trying to change an organization so it supports a totally new paradigm of business and management may appear to be an almost unsurmountable problem. No wonder *In Search of Excellence* and other books with snap-on solutions sell so well. Yet the latest research demonstrates that although the management concepts defined by Peters and Waterman are perfectly valid, those concepts may not be the true priorities for a company seeking success in today's markets. In an article in the

Academy of Management's *Executive* magazine, Michael Hitt and Duane Ireland found that few of Peters and Waterman's "excellent" firms outperformed the average of the *Fortune* 1,000, and quite a number of firms outperformed the "excellent" ones without exhibiting many of the attributes identified by Peters and Waterman. Hitt and Ireland concluded that Peters and Waterman's study, like so many others of the early 1980s, failed to provide managers and consultants with realistic timetables and the sufficiently strong solutions required to resolve deep issues. Even Peters in his latest effort, *Thriving on Chaos*, tends to downplay some of his earlier tenets.

The discipline known as *work design* also offers many quick fixes for organizational problems. Work design is the task of organically pulling functions together into jobs and jobs together into systems that make sense. The principles of scientific management—first developed at the turn of the century by Frederick Taylor and added to in every decade since—have helped us understand work, motivation, cooperation, productivity and a host of related issues. Today, work design represents one of the most important bodies of organization and productivity theory available for consultants.

The basic principles of work design center either on the *Technological Demands* of the work or the *personal needs* of the worker. The technological demands of the work have two aspects: *interdependence* and *task uncertainty*, each of which can be either high or low. In other words, a job can hold a little technological interdependence or a lot. If a job has little interdependence—that is, the work can be done independently from other work—then management should design *individual jobs*. If, on the other hand, the job is interdependent with other jobs, then the organization requires *group design*.

Task uncertainty can also be either high or low. If the uncertainty is low—that is, the work functions are predictable and rote—then *external controls* are appropriate to assure quality

99

and maximum productivity. One person can supervise many workers because all are performing the same functions. If, on the other hand, the uncertainty of the work is high, if new decisions must be made constantly, then a high level of *self-control* is required. In this situation, one person can supervise only three or four individuals because of the variety and frequency of decision making. These two basic aspects of work design are plotted on a matrix on p. 101. The matrix indicates that jobs based on low interdependence and low task uncertainty are individual positions requiring external controls, such as factory jobs. Jobs based on low task uncertainty but higher interdependence still require external control but lend themselves more to groups of workers or teams, such as assembly lines. In the bottom left quadrant, in positions of low interdependence but very high task uncertainty, we tend to find sales people, computer programmers, architects, engineers and academics. This bottom left quadrant could be labeled "professionals." Finally, in the bottom right quadrant, characterized by great interdependence and high uncertainty, is a state of technological job demand that today is seen more frequently and that requires a very special form of work design. It is called *self-design,* an ideal framework to support the flexible, creative, approach to organizational structure required by global markets and global competition today, something I will return to shortly.

The second aspect of work design is *personal worker needs* which, like technological work demands, can be broken down into *social needs* and *order (growth) needs.* Each of these, again, can be be either high or low. If an individual worker has low social needs—that is, he or she doesn't care about teamwork, the company picnic, or building social relationships with co-workers—then obviously an individual job is appropriate. On the other hand, if a worker feels that social interaction, teamwork, the company picnic, and a sense of belonging are very

TECHNOLOGICAL JOB DEMANDS

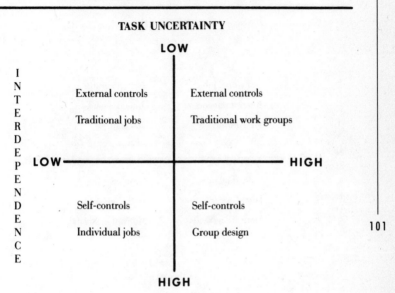

TASK UNCERTAINTY

LOW

INTERDEPENDENCE

| | External controls | External controls |
| | Traditional jobs | Traditional work groups |

LOW ———————————————————————— HIGH

| | Self-controls | Self-controls |
| | Individual jobs | Group design |

HIGH

important to his or her happiness on the job, then a group setting is far more appropriate.

If order needs are low, then the worker has little career ambition and is probably just holding down the job to make enough money to do what he or she really wants to do, whether running a boat on a nearby lake or building model cars. Conversely, for a worker with high order needs (sociologists call them careerists), every rung up the corporate ladder, every handshake from the chairman, every award, certificate, bonus, and title is emotionally critical. These factors appear in the next diagram.

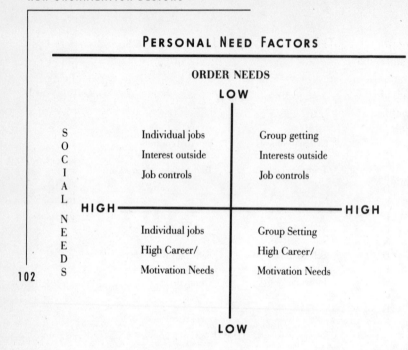

PERSONAL NEED FACTORS

ORDER NEEDS

LOW

S	Individual jobs	Group getting
O	Interest outside	Interests outside
C	Job controls	Job controls
I		
A		
L		

HIGH ———————————————————————— HIGH

N		
E	Individual jobs	Group Setting
E	High Career/	High Career/
D	Motivation Needs	Motivation Needs
S		

LOW

Sociologists and psychologists have known much of this information since the 1970s, but because it did not reach our business schools until the early 1980s, many management consultants who received their training earlier than that are totally unaware of these concepts. They and their clients, in dealing with workers and organizational structures, have been trying to fit round pegs into square holes for years. For example, any number of mildly misanthropic people have perfectly healthy, low social needs, yet employers try to force them into group work settings and insist they attend company picnics. Other employees are told they cannot earn more money unless they take on the responsibility of supervision and management. Often organizations take their best technicians, engineers, or sales personnel and force them into administrative positions where they are doomed to fail, not only because administration is not their natural talent but because, as we have seen here, they prefer jobs with high task uncertainty and tend to resist the predictability of administrative work.

Many consultants may need refresher courses on the latest studies, research, and findings in the area of work design. All will need to work closely with clients to determine at which stage in the organization life cycle the client is currently and which stage will be appropriate over the coming five to seven years. Consultants can help their clients identify which jobs throughout the organization fit into which quadrants of technological demand, and assess which employees hold which personal needs. Such matching of the different factors of work design can drastically improve organizational effectiveness, especially in large organizations. Finally, if most of the rote work in the upper left quadrant can be automated, the organization can reduce its proportion of employees with low social and low order needs. This tends to be the case, for example, in manufacturing companies that have made a heavy investment in robotics and automation. Such companies will be able to keep their brightest, most creative, and best-educated workers to maintain and repair the sophisticated new equipment, while reducing the number of lower-level tasks and workers.

PRINCIPLES OF SELF-DESIGN

Self-design is a broad organization model in which individual divisions or work teams develop personally tailored organization designs. As a management approach, it is designed to maximize employee commitment and involvement both in the way work is organized and in the quality and volume of the output. Self-design originated as an attempt to address how managers approach problem solving, and it has soared to the forefront of management methodology today because of the very nature of the environment in which managers are being forced to manage. As the exponential curve of change forces a new paradigm of management on industry, it also demands this kind of radical new approach to problem solving and innovation.

Many self-design applications have been developed at the University of Southern California's Center for Effective Organizations (CEO) by Tom Cummings and Susan Mohrman. To experience the "Aha!" insight required for self-design, let's begin by recognizing that managers have been solving most of their problems and getting along quite well, thank you, for a very long time, for hundreds of years in fact. In the past thirty to fifty years, sociologists and organization specialists have noted that most successful problem solving is done on the basis of learning how other people solve similar problems. This technique, called *innovation adoption,* works very well whenever there is a clear cause and effect, a clear set of implementable steps, a clear set of instructions, and a straightforward learning process. When you think about it, these conditions are met in about 90 percent of the problems clients have to solve. For example, clients needing a faster computer or a better tool stamping device will generally call friends or peers in the industry, ask what equipment they have been using to resolve the same issues, and call the manufacturer of that equipment. The manufacturer installs the new equipment, trains the employees, and supplies the operating manuals. Mission accomplished, and we're back on the golf course in a week. Why can't everything work that smoothly? The answer is that it can—as long as the problem solving meets the three criteria supplied above.

What happens, though, when management can find no clear cause and effect, there are multiple issues to be resolved, and the goals keep changing as the problem-solving process progresses? Sounds like chaos, doesn't it? Well, this aptly describes the other 10 percent of the problem solving that takes place in organizations, and it is often the most important kind—dealing with *employee attitudes and values*. If we understand generally how people and organizations adopt innovation, we can also understand why it is so hard for them to adopt innovative approaches to delicate and fast-changing issues such as productivity or customer service response time or employee attitudes. What may work in one client firm as a process for improving such issues will not work for another because each company has unique conditions and employees. Quality Circles, for example, are the most abused of all self-design approaches. They have become a buzz-word for employee involvement generally, but they have failed as often as they have succeeded because managers have used them as generic solutions rather than the self-design methods, tailored to each individual department in each unique company, that they should be. Just think about it: the employees in each Quality Circle are different, the problems they deal with are different, management's responses to their suggestions will be different in each organization, and on and on. The process necessary to make Quality Circles work is not Innovation Adoption by any stretch of the imagination.

INSTALLING A SELF-DESIGN PROGRAM

The actual process of self-design begins at the top of the organization and cascades downward from responsibility level to responsibility level. The installation of a self-design program begins with a series of conversations about corporate values, similar to what goes on at a strategic planning retreat. In companies facing aggressive, competitive markets, innovation and entrepreneurship may be highly valued; a health care company or a luxury hotel chain may, instead, value stability and predictability. There are a host of such values to be defined, first by the board and the CEO, later by the executive and senior vice presidents, then by department heads, and eventually by the workers themselves.

At each level, values must be reviewed for relevance to the new, lower level of the organization. In some cases, additional values may be added to those descending from above. In one of my client organizations, for example, senior management claimed that quality of service was the highest corporate value, while staff members in the student loan department cited "mean response time to customers' inquiries" as *their* highest value. At another firm, senior management said it valued entrepreneurship and risk and tolerated failure within the boundaries of experimentation. When branch managers in the organization were interviewed, they reacted differently: "Experimentation? Risk? Why, the last guy permitted an original idea in this branch was ol' Crazy Larry, and they fired him the next day. I think that was back in 1959!"

So the first step in introducing self-design is to cascade values downward throughout the entire organization, testing their interpretation at each level. The second step is to ask each level to evaluate how effectively those values are being realized currently—that is, does the organization at that level act in accordance with its values consistently, occasionally, or not at all? If the values are not consistently realized, then what is getting in the way? In one of our previous examples, the personnel in the student loan department stated that response time was a very important value to them; they also thought they could improve their response times but weren't certain what was preventing such improvement. This leads to the third step in self-design, the development of good data. In the example given, the customer service personnel designed their own questionnaire and sent it to more than 600 customers to get their opinions on how response times, and service generally, could be improved. In other words, the staff members themselves designed a way to better realize the values they had identified as their own.

The fourth step in the self-design process is the replacement of policies and procedures with ones that better support the achievement of the organizational values. Fifth and finally, the group must develop some criteria for periodic measurement so it can evaluate how well it is progressing toward the attainment of its values and goals. As the group meets and surpasses its own standards, it must develop new standards and correspondingly new criteria for measurement. If a particular approach doesn't work, the group tries another. Self-design fosters an organization committed at every level to the same general values and goals, an organization steeped in group approaches, teamwork, trust, openness, and experimentation, with staff members who work for more than just salary and fringe benefits toward the realization of its common values and the achievement of its common goals.

It must be noted, however that self-design produces something very different from the traditional organizations of the past, and a successful program may require as long as three to four years for full implementation. Although some companies, as we saw earlier, have hired HRM staff from leading consulting firms or business schools, many companies—especially machine bureaucracies, where control is more important than creative employee support and development—may lack the kind of skillful and experienced HRM personnel who can take over from the outside consultants as self-design enfolds more and more of the organization. And managers of mature industries—under pressure from Wall Street, shareholders, or mechanistically trained peers—may be reluctant to take the time and manpower required to invest creatively in the future of their organizations through an extensive self-design program.

Self-design remains an avant-garde method of management. It requires consultants go back to school to learn new methodologies and theories and concentrate their energies on helping clients take a longer view of the issues facing them and their enterprises. Extraordinary patience and people skills are needed to succeed with it—but without such skills, consultants probably shouldn't be attempting organization work.

THE SCHMENNER SLOPE

Another organization model of the new paradigm is what I have come to call the *Schmenner Slope*, a model developed by Roger Schmenner of Duke University in 1986, based on earlier work by Dick Chase, director of the Center for Operations Management, Education and Research (COMER) at the University of Southern California. Schmenner's model (originally conceived by Chase to apply to manufacturing companies and beautifully refined by Schmenner for service firms) recognizes that between Mike Porter's lowest-price and value-added strategies there is an entire spectrum of relationships between organizations and their customers. Although Porter cautions managers to commit strategically to one or the other extreme, warning us never to allow our clients to get caught in the middle, Schmenner recognizes that most companies really are on a slope somewhere in between—whether they planned to be there or not and whether they like it or not. Schmenner cautions us to identify where the client's organization is on the slope because each gradient calls for somewhat different organization structures, management issues, and customer relations. A graphic representation of the Schmenner Slope follows.

SCHMENNER'S SLOPE

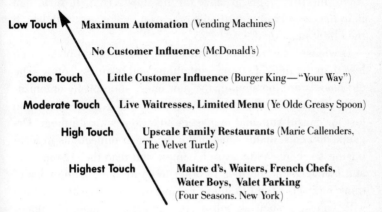

Low Touch **Maximum Automation** (Vending Machines)

No Customer Influence (McDonald's)

Some Touch **Little Customer Influence** (Burger King—"Your Way")

Moderate Touch **Live Waitresses, Limited Menu** (Ye Olde Greasy Spoon)

High Touch **Upscale Family Restaurants** (Marie Callenders, The Velvet Turtle)

Highest Touch **Maitre d's, Waiters, French Chefs, Water Boys, Valet Parking** (Four Seasons. New York)

109

I have chosen the food service business as an example; however, any number of service industries, from banking and insurance to telecommunications or health care, could have been used. At the upper left corner, one finds maximum automation and cheap prices but absolutely no customer input into the products or services. Sloping down, this "low touch" becomes slight touch—as at Burger King, for example, where you can stop the system and custom-make your burger with tomatoes and onions. However, that is still all you are going to get—a burger. Don't try ordering lobster.

The farther down the slope one goes, the more complex the organization must be and the greater its power to respond to customers with custom designs and individual service requirements. Such organizations, of course, are more expensive and diverse, requiring a wider range of products, a more skillful and expensive staff, and so forth. Just as organization consultants must use Greiner's model to identify where their client organizations are on the scale of evolution, so, too, consultants should locate their clients on Schmenner's Slope to identify service management and delivery issues and to address strategically where the firm wants to move on the slope. That, in turn, can help the consultant identify the organizational issues with which the client must deal.

Obviously, the field of organization design is in upheaval no less than the field of strategic planning and business policy. The old models are too simple, the new ones, spun off by organizations seeking rebirth and renewal, are coming at us almost too fast for consultants and managers alike to assimilate them. Organization consultants must make the right connections in local business schools and research centers and read the organization and management journals in order to apply the leading edge of thinking in this field to client organizations and issues. Armed with concepts such as self-design and the Schmenner Slope, consultants of the next decade will be helping managers design the organizations of the twenty-first century.

RECOMMENDED READINGS

Clark, L. H., Jr., "Productivity's Cost: As Manufacturing Firms Gain in Efficiency, They Lag in Adding to Employment," *Wall Street Journal*, Dec. 4, 1986, p. 1.

Cummings, T. G. and R. O. Metzger, "Profitability and the Role of Self-Design: A Banking Application," *National Productivity Review* 6 (3) (Summer 1987).

Fombrun, C. J., et al., *Strategic Human Resource Management* (New York: Wiley, 1984).

King, P., *Performance Planning and Appraisal: A How-to Book for Managers* (New York: McGraw-Hill, 1984).

Lenz, R. T. and M. A. Lyles, "Managing Human Problems in Strategic Planning Systems," *The Journal of Business Strategy* 6 (4) (Spring 1986).

Nadler, L., ed., *The Handbook of Human Resource Development* (New York: Wiley, 1984).

Peters, T., *Thriving on Chaos: Handbook for a Management Revolution* (New York: Alfred A. Knopf, 1988).

Powell, V., *Improving Public Enterprise Performance: Concepts and Techniques* (Geneva: ILO, 1986).

Schmenner, R. W., "How Can Service Businesses Survive and Prosper?" *Sloan Management Review* 27 (3) (Spring 1986).

Schuler, R. S. and S. E. Jackson, "Linking Competitive Strategies with Human Resource Management Practices," *Academy of Management Executive* 1 (3) (August 1987).

Tannenbaum, R., et al., *Human Systems Development* (San Francisco: Jossey Bass, 1985).

Tushman, M. L., et al., "Convergence and Upheaval: Managing the Unsteady Pace of Organizational Evolution," *California Management Review* 29 (1) (Fall 1986).

CHAPTER 7

NEW CHALLENGES IN COMPENSATION

I t will be no surprise that this chapter treats yet another management and consulting discipline currently experiencing radical change. Our systems and practices of compensation and reward, however, are changing in an almost grudging way, one position at a time, one department at a time, one company at a time. It is less a revolution than house-to-house guerilla warfare.

The reason for this is the almost intransigent position of managers, who have been genetically imprinted with mechanistic values that dictate that people should be paid according to their rank and position in the hierarchy, their tenure with the organization, and their education. This system has ruled for well over 150 years so that now any other is virtually inconceivable, especially one in which compensation is linked directly to one's contribution to profits regardless of rank, title, longevity, or education. Seriously altering such a system would be pretty scary for a manager who has learned over the past twenty years that, as a rule, senior vice presidents earn 25 percent more than vice presidents and employees ought to receive an automatic 3 percent increase for each additional year of service. It is even more threatening when first heard as a senior vice president if the executive functions in the organization are so ill defined that it is not clear what kind or level of performance is expected of each senior manager.

REWARD SYSTEMS OF THE MACHINE BUREAUCRACY

The traditional machine bureaucracy formulas for pay and reward systems are still taught today in management programs and at leading universities and business schools across the country. Basically, they begin with the classic compensation committee of the board, which is charged with reviewing corporate pay and fringes every two years or so to "assure that the organization maintains a leadership position in its industry to attract and retain the best and the brightest" or some such catechism. This process includes

- Pay policy and authorities (where salary decisions are made),
- Job analysis (salary justification),
- Job descriptions,
- Determining the relative worth of a job,
- External influences,
- Concepts of pay relevance in the industry and in the area.

All of the above establish a pay system based on one's position relative to the CEO and to one's peers in the industry or in the geographic area. For example, in many industries it is *de rigeur* for the "second highest paid officer" in the organization to be paid approximately 75 percent of the salary of "the highest paid officer." The "third highest paid officer" would be paid 55 to 60 percent of the salary of "the highest paid officer," and so forth, with all managerial salaries keyed to that of the CEO. Further, the CEOs salary is based roughly on the size of that firm in its industry. CEO's of firms half as large make half as much, and CEOs of firms twice as large, make approximately twice as much. With neat mathematical formulas such as these for salary grades, consultants of the old school could draw lovely exponential curves through the midpoint salaries of each progressive grade and point to the resultant geometric art work as an "acid test" that the pay grades created were proper and in order!

Usually, a major policy manual follows, describing the procedures for administering annual salary reviews, developing salary budgets, and implementing salary increases. These were (and still are) replete with paranoid admonitions not to review all nonexempt personnel at the same time, say, at the end of the year, to avoid workers' comparing increases with profits and ending up unionizing, and iterating the need for the strict enforcement of salary secrecy, to avoid employees' learning just how irrationally salary decisions are made.

What this traditional compensation approach produces, according to leading observers of the discipline such as Rosabeth Moss Kanter, is an upwelling of outrage and anger on the part of employees, who feel used, abused, and manipulated by the same senior managers who continue to pay themselves virtually unlimited amounts of money.

■ **CASE IN POINT**

Recently a student of mine who works during the day for Federal Express noted angrily that many of the employee benefits that Fred Smith developed when he started the company are now being reduced or, in the case of the employee picnic, that workers are being asked to pay for benefits out of their own pocket. My student can understand the need for Federal Express to reduce costs, but she is angry that while these cost reduction steps are affecting her and her colleagues negatively, senior management continues to pay itself more money each year. Her anger is very real.

Overall, this outrageous system is not based on a simple, direct link between salary and profit contribution. Instead, traditionalists and their bureaucratic approaches to compensation have set the stage for an *Alice in Wonderland* tea party. For if salary is a statistical exercise based on the CEO's compensation and linked to what other CEOs in the industry are paid, then an individual employee's performance is irrelevant to the reward system. This means that any careerist in personnel administration can make salary adjustments even though he or she is ten departments removed from the employee affected and that supervisors and managers may not even be involved in salary review decisions concerning their immediate subordinates. The inflexible logic of such a system not only removes managers from the decision-making process, but also determines that the process of assuring competitive salaries is a process of watching other firms in the industry and adjusting to their changes rather than watching one's own bottom line.

PAY FOR PERFORMANCE

Fortunately, this absurd situation is changing. A significant number of U.S. workers in private enterprise now receive compensation based on their direct impact on profits; and according to federal government statistics, upward of a half million American companies now have some form of profit sharing. Almost all consultants, whether independents or members of large consulting organizations (the sort of people for whom I am writing this book), have always been compensated on a direct pay-for-performance system. And certainly all the millions of self-employed people in the United States are compensated in this way. Yet even with so many familiar examples of direct profit sharing or pay-for-performance before us, only about 25 percent of all American workers are exposed to such organic programs.

It's such a simple concept! The new, creative theory of compensation mandates that employees—managers and hourly workers alike—should be compensated relative to their direct contribution to the profits of the company (*profit sharing*) and, in some cases, that specific groups or teams of employees should be rewarded not only for their direct contribution to profits but also for their efforts in reducing expenses (*gain sharing*). But if it's such a simple concept, why aren't more companies, especially *Fortune* 1,000 firms, adopting it wholeheartedly?

The answer seems to lie back with that same concept of denial that we discussed in the beginning of the book. In other words, Housekeepers cannot accept that employees want to be compensated in any way other than the traditional system. Before clients adopt a system of pay-for-performance, they have to make two difficult conceptual readjustments to how they look at compensation generally. The first apparently "new" concept is that pay should have no relationship to position or title except in relation to the effect the individual has on company earnings. This concept immediately destroys the logic by which they traditionally identify who is important, who has the power, and who commands respect; and it throws a great deal of the old mechanistic framework into doubt. How do you evaluate whether senior management is contributing to the bottom line if its *collective* job is to plan, motivate, direct, and lead? These crucial management responsibilities may appear to be unquantifiable and thus nonrewardable under the new way of thinking. Then, there is the understandable reluctance of the generation currently coming into power to change the old system *now*. These people had to wait their turn for twenty years or more, while they put up with all the inequities of the old system. Now, finally, it is *their* turn. Who has the right to take that away from them with some "radical" new compensation program?

The second new concept involves a recognition that if one is to be compensated for one's contribution to earnings, then the person best suited to evaluate that contribution is one's immediate supervisor or manager, not the director of personnel, the executive vice president, or even the owner of the company, six levels removed. This change, in turn, has tremendous emotional traps in it. Power in the company shifts dramatically from one of title and hierarchy, usually based on longevity, to one of direct line supervision, based on functional performance.

Consultants in this field may often create as many problems as they solve by promoting the mechanistic compensation systems they learned ten or fifteen years ago. Even when consultants attempt to bring innovative concepts to their clients, they must overcome the obstacles of industry tradition and entrenched organizational power before they can set things right. Jeffrey Kerr and John Slocum of SMU note that reward systems reflect corporate cultures. They identify two different types of reward systems: The Corporate Hierarchy System and The Performance-Based System. The former reflects a "clan-like" culture that resists any changes to traditional compensation methods or values, while the latter reflects a "market" culture that pushes to reward the top performers. In their research, Kerr and Slocum point to aluminum, forest products, utilities, and pharmaceuticals as typical of the first group and diversified consumer and industrial products as industries typical of the latter.

118

This market approach to compensation also requires that if employees are to be rewarded based on their contributions to earnings, then to a greater or lesser degree management must allow subordinates more latitude in how they manage and operate in their areas of responsibility. This includes how they organize themselves and their work. Again, the new compensation tends to shift authority away from the traditional power base. But it is the looser, organic entrepreneurial values that help to identify and develop new earnings opportunities. Perhaps this is one of the reasons that so many large companies are encouraging *intrapreneurship*, and setting up independent suborganizations to develop new concepts, ideas, and products— suborganizations that cannot be held back by machine bureaucracy approaches to pay, rewards, and organization.

PROFIT AND GAIN SHARING

Many ways are emerging for employees to share in a firm's profits, from once-a-year bonuses based on audited and tax-massaged results (the worst approach) to quarterly team incentives based on predetermined operational performance standards (one of the best approaches). Some companies have complex stock option plans—such as Lincoln Electric, where the employees' biggest bonus in some years is their stock dividend—while other firms award a combination of stock and cash. What is important about these programs is that they demonstrate that people who contribute a great deal to earnings earn a great deal. Workers (and managers) who do not contribute as much are treated less generously, and those that cannot contribute meaningfully are not kept on the payrolls at all. Further, as systems and processes become more complex every year, individuals are more often parts of teams or task forces. These teams and departments working well together determine a firm's financial successes; therefore, it is the team, task force, or the department members who should share in earnings on a fairly equal basis.

Gain sharing merely takes the entire concept one step further. If a department's operating budget is, say, $500,000 for the year, and the team comes in $75,000 (15 percent) under budget at year end, those cost savings flow directly to the bottom line. The department then shares directly in those added earnings, with as much as 30 to 50 percent of the amount divided among the department members. Many firms on quarterly profit sharing have performance goals or expense budgets posted so that employees can evaluate how they are doing against their earnings or cost-saving objectives. Such simple methods of performance communication keep a positive tension among team and department members, give employees an ongoing awareness of what is really driving the firm, and encourage employees to devise new ways to meet or surpass objectives.

DETERMINING STANDARDS OF PERFORMANCE

Perhaps the greatest barrier to effective profit-sharing programs is the alleged difficulty firms have in determining and establish-

119

ing meaningful performance criteria or *standards of performance*. The solution to this problem, of course, rests with the firm's own employees, who know what excellent, good, and poor performance is among peers at every level. But management seldom thinks of asking workers. As a consultant in this area, one of my functions has been to work with employees in developing such performance standards, always to the amazement and chagrin of management. The same holds true in dealing with the problem of high turnover and absenteeism.

■CASE IN POINT

In a major San Francisco client suffering from unacceptable levels of turnover, we established that the most stable employees were the Filipino workers. We asked them to search among their friends and relatives for others who might be qualified to perform the work in question. The result was a steady increase among Filipinos as employees and a rapid decline in absenteeism and error rates!

Employees can offer a wealth of solutions to operating problems when they are asked. The tragedy is that they are seldom asked. In the establishment of performance standards, they are often tougher on themselves than their supervisors would be. Allowing them to help determine what the standards ought to be provides them with ownership in those standards and the organizational values they reflect; and this, in turn, prevents them from rejecting the performance-based reward system. Without cooperation, performance-based compensation cannot be developed fully. Every position in the organization must have standards established for it.

Another area of difficulty in establishing such standards has to do with staff positions. What exactly is an advertising manager or corporate legal counsel or the director of personnel administration supposed to do? Just how many letters should an executive secretary type to be productive? What if the boss is away and she has no letters to type? How are these issues to be measured and criteria developed? Consultants versed in this area know that in highly profit-conscious organizations, staff functions operate as if outside service firms were their rivals. For example, in the area of marketing, how many new accounts were generated as a result of the last ad campaign, or how much were sales improved? If the ad was purely for image, what was the effect on image? Did recognition of the company logo increase? By how much? At what cost? Are the regional and branch managers satisfied with the support they are getting from the marketing department? If they had separate budgets and the authority to hire local marketing consultants, would they continue to use the marketing department or would they hire outside firms?

In the area of human resource management, how much has turnover been reduced in the past two years? What about absenteeism? Just how good is employee product knowledge or cross-selling skills? There are many standards to set and hold personnel management accountable for in a profit-driven firm. Obviously, when such criteria are set for the first time, there will be tremendous resistance, weeping, wailing, and long dissertations as to why it can never work—but it does and it will. Consultants must ask their clients a fundamental question: Are you really committed to higher profits? Your clients may talk a good line (all executives do), but more than casual involvement is required to make this system work.

The difference between involvement and commitment is like a ham and egg breakfast. The hen was involved, the pig was committed!

When all the secrecy is peeled off and all members of the organization must justify their performance, great and exciting things can happen. Workers share the stresses of managers, and managers learn to trust employees. Everything that is unimportant to the job at hand is discarded. A number of firms have taken to posting all salaries and salary increases. This confirms that there are no secrets and communicates an important piece of information: Here's who's doing a top job and here's what that can mean around here—an added incentive for those who aren't pulling their weight. Some firms go so far as to have employees submit their requests for salary increases to their section or department, and employees vote whether or not the applicant deserves an increase. Talk about peer pressure! But there is so much to be discarded from the old methods in the area of pay and compensation that the whole subject is sometimes painful even to discuss. In some mature companies, it may take another generation of management before the New Compensation takes hold.

IMPROVING PERFORMANCE AND COPING WITH CHANGE

How can consultants help their clients in this critical area? The answer lies in another of those contradictions that fill the industry. On the one hand, process approaches seem to be the most effective in helping clients recognize how drastically they must change; but on the other, a content approach is required to construct profit- or gain-sharing programs and stock option plans. In fact, if your client is a public company, a good corporate attorney familiar with SEC and IRS regulations should be a member of this change team. It is not feasible to cover all the details of profit-sharing and stock option plans in a book like this, but I do want to discuss a broader issue: how consultants can help clients deal with, accept, and eventually relish changes of this magnitude.

Twenty years ago, when Management-by-Objectives (MBO) was "hot" and some of us were recommending it as a management style, one of its principal selling points was that, in place of two or three very senior executives worrying about earnings, with MBO, as many as ten to twelve key people were involved with and personally concerned about earnings. With three to four times as many people devoted to the issues, the outcome had to be better. And for those companies that kept their MBO simple and straightforward, the results often were far better. Profit sharing is no different, but this principle works on a much grander scale. With a good profit-sharing scheme, every employee, from the CEO to the "gofer" on the loading dock, is concerned about earnings and what can affect profits. It makes for smarter employees—people who do more than just put in their time.

123

When talking to clients, I describe such a scenario and ask how they expect to compete against firms committed to profit-sharing programs. I also ask what they believe it will take to outperform such an organization. The answer, of course, is a company whose employees are equally involved and dedicated. That leads to the (hopeful) conclusion on the part of the client that profit sharing is a formidable competitive weapon.

Another part of this discussion rides on the recognition that many older managers feel disenfranchised at the loss of some of their status and authority as a result of pay-for-performance programs. These managers must be counseled and, in many cases, provided with some extra assistance in discovering ways to regain the prestige or authority they perceive they have lost. In turn, a classic step in getting nay-sayers to support a new program is to involve them in the initial meetings or allow them places on various committees formed to establish performance criteria or develop bonus payouts, and so forth.

Consultants also are needed to help develop overall approaches to client productivity improvement and to develop innovative approaches to specific performance problems such as alcoholism. Clients will often see enormous performance improvements simply through the implementation of a pay-for-performance program, and in many firms you can make a big difference by allowing managers and supervisors across different regions or plants to share their experiences.

■ CASE IN POINT

A few years ago, one of my clients had remarkable success by offering lunch on the company for the best section attendance recorded each month. The section with the best attendance record for the quarter won lunch in the boardroom with the chairman, with no supervisors allowed! The competition for these inexpensive lunches and the eventual private meeting with the chairman became so intense after awhile that the firm's greatest problem was employees ill with flu and high fever who came to work so as not to let their sections down!

124

COMPENSATION AND CORPORATE RENEWAL

All of this leads back to the question of the role of consultants in this challenging area. We have noted that consultants must approach compensation with both process- and content-oriented approaches. Consultants can act also as catalysts, gathering and sharing knowledge from many parts of the organization about what is working and what is not and, among various companies, about productivity programs and specific problem solving. The implementation of a profit- and gain-sharing program for a client involves an enormous amount of front-end labor to develop performance criteria, operational objectives to be tracked, and even the tracking systems themselves. Once the program is in place, you will have to work with the managers to ensure their commitment to the concept and with the supervisors to minimize the stress they will feel at having their competence continually tested.

Finally, I want to say a word about personnel selection. One of the principal reasons companies are working so hard to develop new compensation systems as part of an overall program of rebirth and renewal is to attract and retain "the best and the brightest." Marc Gerstein and Heather Reisman, of Gerstein, Reisman & Associates in Toronto, have done seminal research into the characteristics of managers required to perform certain leadership roles in differing situations: new ventures, maintaining the status quo, retrenching, dynamic growth, and so forth. What they found agrees strongly with Clarke and Pratt's contentions discussed in Chapter 1. Gerstein and Reisman note that in each of their eight different scenarios developed from actual case histories, quite different leadership and managerial traits and experience—strengths, if you will—were needed. Therefore, they suggest that employers evaluate job openings carefully and assess the management traits required before developing the job description itself. Then they should develop a profile of the correct leader before undertaking a search.

For similar reasons, Competency Testing is back again. It was used frequently in the early 1980s and its values are being proven substantial a decade later. Competency Testing takes Gerstein and Reisman's theme all the way down to the bottom of the organization, attempting to identify a particular set of motives, traits, and social skills for each job in the organization. Specialists can be trained to identify and search for these competencies, and the result is higher employee performance and morale, and far less turnover.

LEARNING THE ROPES

Because of the complexity of the issues and organizational details of compensation, consultants interested in this evolving field must network heavily with colleagues and peers, especially from the tax and legal disciplines. Those issues and those details will vary not only from company to company and industry to industry, and among various forms of ownership, but also from state to state. Further, this entire area rests on shifting sands. The 1986 Tax Reform Act did away with the corporate tax deduction for company-sponsored employee stock option plans. As a result, many firms revised or did away with these programs in 1987 and 1988. The exciting part of the new compensation is the opportunity to link it with methods of self-design and many of the other new organizational and behavioral change programs that are taking over and will become SOP between now and the next century. The results will be entire organizations working smarter, not harder.

126

RECOMMENDED READINGS

Bennis, W., and B. Nanus, *Leaders: The Strategies for Taking Charge* (New York: Harper & Row, 1985).

Eichel, E., and H. E. Bender, *Performance Appraisal: A Study of Current Techniques* (New York: American Management Associates, 1984).

Gerstein, M., and H. Reisman, "Strategic Selection: Matching Executives to Business Conditions," *Sloan Management Review* (Winter 1983).

Goleman, D., "The New Competency Tests: Matching the Right People to the Right Jobs," *Psychology Today* (January 1981).

Henderson, R. I., *Compensation Management: Rewarding Performance* (Reston, Va.: Reston Publishing Co., 1985).

Herzberg, F., "One More Time: How Do You Motivate Employees?," *Harvard Business Review* 65 (5) (Sept.-Oct. 1987).

Kantor, R. M., "The Attack on Pay," *Harvard Business Review* 65 (2) (March-April 1987).

Kerr, J., and J. W. Slocum, Jr., "Managing Corporate Culture through Reward Systems," *Academy of Management Executive* 1 (2) (May 1987).

Kerr, S., "On the Folly of Rewarding A, While Hoping for B," *Academy of Management Journal* 18 (4) (Dec. 1975).

Quarry, M., et al., *Taking Stock: Employee Ownership at Work* (Cambridge, Mass.: Ballinger, 1986).

Rosen, C., and M. Quarrey, "How Well Is Employee Ownership Working?," *Harvard Business Review* 65 (5) (Sept.-Oct. 1987).

Schuster, J. R., *Management Compensation in High Technology Companies: Assuring Corporate Excellence* (Lexington, Mass.: Lexington Books, 1984).

Schuster, M., "Gain Sharing: Doing It Right the First Time," *Sloan Management Review* 28 (2) (Winter 1987).

■

CHAPTER 8

NEW

MARKETING

SERVICES

■

OUTMODED THINKING

Marketing is an enormously broad field, ranging from market research (which itself includes over a dozen basic forms of research), to packaging design (which, in some cases, is but one step away from fine art). For the purposes of this chapter, I will be referring to consulting services in strategic marketing and its basic components—product development, sales, and distribution. This field, like the others we have looked at, is one in which inflexible, mechanistic models have too often replaced genuine creativity. One of the most popular traditional marketing frameworks was the *Vector Analysis*, which follows.

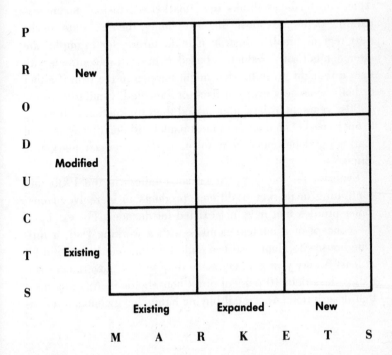

By working with their clients to fill in the squares on this matrix, consultants attempted to help their clients extend their product lines and markets. The problem with this and other traditional models is that they encouraged American managers to sell in concentric circles, teaching them to extend their markets one step and one product at a time, and did nothing to encourage global thinking. Americans need such encouragement, for they tend to be more provincial in outlook than almost any other nationality in the world today. Alabamans look down on Mississippians, and Mississippians feel superior to Alabamans; third-generation Californians from San Francisco feel superior to anyone residing south of Daly City; and old money from Boston, Philadelphia, and Richmond still can't wait for the interlopers to go home so they can get on with being the unofficial royalty of the land. With a general view of the world that is already compartmentalized, it is not surprising that a large segment of American business thinks that "market expansion" means expanding to the next town, the next county, the next state, or the next region. Small industrial manufacturers, for example, are often content with production based on one or two contracts with nary a thought given to what might happen to the firm if either or both customers ever cut back or canceled. Similarly, in the 1980s, years after deregulation and the introduction of banking to open-market competition, most banks still don't have a formal marketing department or a full-time, experienced marketing officer.

Even worse, too many American retailers in the 1980s are continuing to market traditional products to stereotyped customer profiles that have not existed for decades. For example, the concept of a nuclear family—with a working Dad, a full-time housewife Mom, and two children—has not been valid for at least twenty years. Today, according to U.S. government statistics, less than 10 percent of all households in America meet that description. And retail buying habits have changed just as drastically in the past decade, although some executives appear not to have noticed. The typical modern household (65 percent of which have both partners working) is "time bankrupt"—that is, lacks the time to shop or run errands except before 8:00 A.M. and after 5:00 P.M. No wonder telemarketing and computer shopping are becoming popular and credit cards are now often "pre-authorized" and sold by mail. Discount brokerage and savings accounts located across country and managed through late-night telephone lines are becoming more typical than atypical. Most depositors seldom visit their bank branch during the week anymore.

> ■**C**ASE IN POINT
> To help deal with these rapidly changing market needs, BancOne in the Midwest has reduced its branch staffing levels during the week to absolute minimums while providing fully staffed branch offices all day Saturday and Sunday. The demand has been so overwhelming that a typical Sunday line for service is out the door!

131

In California, the home of drive-in everything, no new drive-up banking facilities have been built by any of the major banks in years. People are too busy to swing by in the middle of the day to use them, and because they require separate staff, they are no longer practical to operate. End of an era!

AMERICAN PRODUCTS AND FOREIGN TASTES

Consultants, who should have known better, have in fact been guilty of perpetuating this outmoded thinking. Many consultants sold market research based on two premises—first, that the next market expansion was the nearest concentric circle, and second, that demographics more than psychographics held the answers clients needed. Such mechanistic solutions can extend sales briefly to the extent that expanded geographic markets and mildly modified products add longevity to any product line, but most of the top marketing consultants of the 1970s (and many still in the 1980s) missed what was really happening: the emergence of global markets and globally marketable consumer products.

According to the Department of Commerce, 85 percent of all U.S. exports are generated by a mere 250 companies!

132

So far, comparatively few export efforts have been made; and many of those have been dismal failures. The first and greatest problem, I think, has been in the area of overseas market research, an area where consultants should have been able to help. Although the Common Market countries have always kept excellent data, and each country within this economic alliance has outstanding statistics arising both from industry trade associations and from government agencies, many technically developing nations—or LDCs (less developed countries), as the banks call them—have poor and very unreliable statistics at best. Often the only way to obtain such data is painfully time consuming and very expensive. As a result, Americans traditionally have not had the patience or the budgets to find out what they need to know in any but the most developed markets.

Worse, there has been an almost total lack of product and customer research even in the most developed countries. The Housekeeper mentality and the reluctance to depart from established routine tend to take over, and companies begin exporting products without any modifications to acknowledge foreign tastes, customs, or worse, foreign electrical circuitry. Many

American products are exported without a translation of the user's or maintenance manuals or instruction booklets; at $20 to $25 per page translation costs, many smaller firms just wistfully hope their customers can read English. Yet there isn't a foreign product sold in America that doesn't have an English language version of its directions for use. Some major firms with multiple export products have a need for as many as 200,000-page translations a year, and as foreign languages often run longer in typesetting, they also have to redesign their brochures. A few firms now have internal translation staffs, but this luxury begins to pay for itself only after about 5,000 pages per year. However it is handled, this remains an essential consideration for doing business in the global market. Electrical systems must be changed to 220V, instructions and brochures translated and even redesigned, packaging changed, and even a product's name often must be altered for foreign markets.

133

■CASE IN POINT

Some American financiers formed a private investment bank in Munich years ago. They wanted to call it Orbis Bank, meaning "the bank of the world." They even went as far as to select its logo—*ob.* What they didn't do but should have done at the time was check with the German bureau of trademarks. If they had done so, they would have found that *ob* was the logo of the then largest-selling West German brand of women's tampon. Instead, they just forged ahead assuming "their" logo was unique and wasted tens of thousands of dollars.

Americans also tend to shoot themselves in the foot in the area of bank support. Not only are most U.S. firms unable to cope with a simple international letter of credit, but few American banks provide any form of international banking services to their customers. If you live in New York, Miami or Los Angeles, fine! But try to get a letter of credit in Singapore dollars or Greek drachmas if your firm is in Omaha or Little Rock. To rely on small community banks and bankers to handle unfamiliar international trade contracts for managers inexperienced in the drill is asking the blind to lead the blind.

■ **CASE IN POINT**

To help smaller U.S. firms deal with these financing issues, the federal government (in the indirect form of the U.S. Export-Import Bank) is sponsoring major pilot projects in Columbus, Ohio, Tucson, Arizona, and Los Angeles in which it provides specialists to lead would-be exporters through the maze of paperwork involved in international loans—thus, in effect, getting into the consulting business.

Most frustrating of all, American consumer and retail products are failing to succeed in global markets because they have lost their reputation for quality. Shoddy products have never sold well anywhere in the world. Moreover, American export efforts are hampered generally by the mechanistic, short-term orientation of American managers and by our government's lemming-like urge to export its own puritanical ethics. The pressures from senior management, owners, and analysts to constantly outperform the previous quarter places American companies in a difficult situation. In opening any foreign market, it may take years to establish a foothold, learn the best merchandising techniques, or consummate a partnership with the right distributors. In other areas, especially in LDCs, it is difficult to know whether the country will remain politically and economically stable over the ensuing three to five years it may take for a firm to establish its product and earn back its start-up costs. Moreover, agency fees, and many other such payments or *baksheesh* are standard features of business throughout the world, except in the United States. If U.S. enterprises really want to succeed in other markets, is it wise to insist that everyone else play by America's rules? This is an unrealistic and provincial morality that has helped foreign competitors gain market share from U.S. companies in ever-larger bites simply because, in many international markets, no one wants to do business that way. There's no money in it!

JOINT VENTURES AND CREATIVE DISTRIBUTION

Clearly, we need a new marketing model that takes account of the complexities of the global market for industrial and retail consumer products. Both product categories can be effectively developed and marketed on a global basis through intricate international partnership agreements—to research, design, and manufacture and also to distribute, sell, and service. Kenichi Ohmae perhaps summarizes it best with his concept of *triad power*. He states simply, but forcefully, that there are three principal markets in the world today: Europe, Japan, and the United States. The three are locked integrally into one another with respect to product development, manufacturing facilities and processes, marketing, and sales. Ohmae makes these contentions on the basis that no one firm, not even General Motors, can afford the "cost of entry" to perform the R&D, tooling, design, and start-up required to produce a product that has worldwide markets and appeal. In fact, even if one such company could be found, it would have to be mechanistic and highly inefficient. What we find developing worldwide is a series of organic, flexible international partnerships between Japanese and American and American and European and European and Japanese firms, whereby new products are designed off joint-venture technology for global—not national, regional, or local—

135

consumption. These products, in turn, are marketed through creative joint-venture distribution agreements in the three principal markets, Japan, America, and Western Europe. In order to accomplish these objectives, many of the world's largest industrial firms have been forging joint-ventures with each other over the past decade or acquiring key smaller companies abroad where R&D, technology, or design is unique.

Examples of such partnerships are endless. In the automotive industry, acquisitions familiar to most of us include Chrysler's purchase of Aston Martin, GM's purchase of Lotus Cars, the GM-Nissan joint venture known as NUMI, whose mission it is to build a small, economy car for GM in the United States. Ford also has many international subsidiaries, not the least of which include Ford of England, Ford of Germany, Lamborghini in Italy, and Ford of Australia. But the internationalization of industry goes far beyond the automotive industry. It includes General Electric's acquisition of Thomson medical equipment in France in exchange for Thomson's acquisition of GE's consumer products division, including RCA-TV back in 1987; Mercedes-Benz's expansion out of automotive engineering and into high tech electronics and design through several recent purchases; Pechiney, the state-owned French copper company, merging with Societa Metallurgica Italiana to form Europe's largest copper group; Thomson of France, again, buying Thorn EMI's consumer electronics operations; and Sweden's Electrolux, which already owns Italy's Zanussi, acquiring Thorn EMI's kitchen appliance division in 1987. The list goes on and on. In addition to Thomson's agreement with GE, in the past five years Thyssen, Hoechst, ICI, Rhone Poulence, BASF, Elf Acquitaine, and Renault all have made major acquisitions in the United States. But so, too, have Nissan, Honda, and nine of the ten largest Japanese banks.

In 1987, the *Harvard Business Review* surveyed key opinion leaders around the world on the issue of this new global competitiveness. The report shows that a number of nations see international trade as a way to strengthen their economic clout in the world community. As the HBR reported, "This is not traditional mercantilism, in which a country exports to buy and hold gold, but a new form, in which exports help gain market share and move the country upscale technologically to higher value-added items in order to gain economic and technological power."

At the retail level, where R&D seldom requires the billions necessary to develop new automobile, aircraft or rail technologies (or the development of radically new technologies such as superconductivity), existing products previously sold only regionally or nationally hold great promise if marketed effectively on an international basis. But American managers must realize that marketing globally is totally different from marketing nationally or locally. There are different methods of sales and distribution, and of financing and payment, but all are well worth the effort to learn if strong market potential can be identified.

Unfortunately, what many American firms have attempted to do is maintain their control by developing their own captive sales force overseas, not realizing that in many countries sales personnel are not paid exclusively on commission; that in some, fourteen months' salary is the law; and that in others still, once a person is engaged, he or she cannot be terminated without government approval. Just as the United States has developed some very restrictive and difficult labor laws over the last two decades, so, too, have other nations, and many of those countries have had centuries to work on the nuances. To even think of developing captive overseas sales and distribution is sheer folly.

What many successful companies have done is locate successful agents, importers, and distributors—legitimate people handling only top-quality products. The real sale, then, is to those foreign marketeers needed to handle the product in question. They become the single-sale customer. Once such marketeers are convinced that American efforts are sincere and legitimate, the product of quality, the supply readily available on an exclusive basis, and the price excitingly competitive, they will willingly negotiate an agency or wholesale agreement. That the American company has no control over the end salesforce and that the importer doesn't speak fluent English should be secondary issues.

Another method used even more frequently today is for a manufacturer with its own distribution system in, say, America to locate a foreign market in, say, Japan, and then draw up a mutually beneficial trade and exchange agreement whereby the Japanese manufacturer will receive exclusive rights to distribute the American product in the Far East. In return, the American company, through its distribution system, will receive exclusive rights to distribute products of the Japanese firm in North America. (A hundred years ago, one would simply say, "You scratch my back, I'll scratch yours." Today, it takes six lawyers and four interpreters.)

138

OLIVETTI—A NEW ROLE MODEL

Of all the companies involved in global markets and global competition, the Italian firm of Olivetti is the most striking example of what needs to be done for a firm to survive into the twenty-first century. Olivetti's marketing strategy is based precisely on what we have been recommending: the *formation of alliances*. As recently as the late 1970s, Olivetti was thought of as an old-line typewriter company, and a rather obsolete one at that. It had corporate debt in excess of ten times its total capital and prospects looked grim. Then Carlo De Benedetti came to the rescue. Taking over management of the company, he completely turned it around in just seven years! By 1985, Olivetti had a return on sales of more than 8 percent, 67 percent of its sales were outside Italy, 50 percent of its revenues were coming from products and services that had not existed five years previously—and all with 18,000 fewer workers than in 1980.

To accomplish this, De Benedetti developed and negotiated a system of alliances for Olivetti that, while they gave away major holdings in the firm, created so large a pie that Olivetti's remaining slice still was much greater than anything previously held. The alliances began in 1979 with the sale of 50 percent of the company to AT&T, a major coup. In return for access to U.S. markets, capital, and technology, Olivetti offered AT&T access to key European markets. In 1985, Olivetti sold an additional 20 percent of its shares to Toshiba for access to Asian markets and ease of modification of its products for Asia while offering Toshiba additional entry to European markets. Olivetti then purchased a 22 percent stake in Pelikan, the Swiss stationery supply company; and for another 5 percent of Olivetti stock, picked up Triumph/Adler, the German typewriter manufacturer, from Volkswagen, principally for the access that company provided Olivetti in Germany. Out of all this maneuvering for alliances, Olivetti has learned there is a basic contradiction to successful global marketing.

While everyone cannot be all things, a firm cannot exist on niches alone.

Olivetti sees itself in the field of Information Technology and perceives itself as Market Needs Driven. The firm has developed over thirty venture capital operations since 1979 and sees several of them beginning to pay off a decade later. Olivetti's

139

marketing managers understand that their company must participate in all three major global markets and that the alliance
strategy offers the only opportunity to become an international
"GE" and survive. Daimler-Benz and Westinghouse recently
formed such a strategic alliance to produce and market railway
systems and equipment, and the game goes on. In 1992, all
trade barriers between Common Market countries come down,
and with this, open markets and international alliances will be
the norm, and solo company efforts the exception.

MACRO- AND MICRO- LEVEL ASSISTANCE

140   Consultants can help their client firms learn their crucial lessons in a variety of ways. In large organizations, there probably
is some global marketing sophistication and even some international alliances already in place. But they still may need help
unlocking traditional thinking, especially in identifying the export potential of products in smaller subsidiaries and affiliates
and in the ongoing search to find new global alliances that mesh
well with the overall strategic marketing plans. These are easy
statements to make, but it is far more difficult to use them to
gain inroads to prospective firms as a consultant. The key, it
seems to me, is the development by the consultant and the consulting firm of their own strong international alliances. Such
alliances, on the other hand, are far easier to develop than it
may seem. For example, there are a host of international consulting organizations throughout Europe that are always interested in meeting U.S. consultants. In the past few years on trips
to Europe for completely different reasons, I have initiated
strong new friendships with consultants in England, Holland,
Italy and Denmark. With many European industrial firms acquiring American companies at bargain basement prices these

days, eventually your friendship with a European consultant could mean a new client for you here!

With such international contacts, a consultant is in a good position to offer U.S. clients everything from European-based market research to plant site selection and to use such alliances to establish industrial client networks. A second opportunity to provide marketing assistance is the field of global marketing strategy itself. Which products are globally marketable today, which ones might be obsolesced in six months, and which new products should be brought to market in six, twelve, and twenty-four months? Just being able to develop a thorough international marketing checklist—from owner's manual translations to package design and bill of lading explanations—could be surprisingly helpful to certain divisions of even the largest and supposedly most sophisticated corporations.

At the other end of the spectrum, there are thousands of independent consultants and consultants in smaller partnerships who can help small to midsized American companies establish specific export programs or act as specialists to large clients. These companies need basic assistance such as the translation of owner's manuals and package designs, but consultants also can help in finding bankers willing to work with their smaller clients in international trade or in locating overseas contacts for market research. Consultants developing seminars for smaller companies also have every reason to hope for success. They must be pragmatic, include guest speakers who can talk about their own successes, and devote some significant time to international finance, currency risk, and import-export financing and payments, the biggest bugaboo of all for small companies.

For all the potential problems and complexities, foreign markets are ready and waiting for American goods and services. They are just waiting for clients aggressive enough to find the consultants with sufficient knowledge to make the exports happen.

The United States complains about the balance of trade with Japan but in fact, IBM does about $6 billion in sales there annually, Coca-Cola has 70 percent of the Japanese soft drink market, and U.S. companies and their overseas subsidiaries sell more than $44 billion a year worth of goods and services to Japan.

Companies that are already sensitive to strong competition in the areas of quality and service should have only minor problems in developing their international markets. But manufacturers who still believe they can foist second-class merchandise off on the rest of the world, as though buyers abroad are somehow less competent than U.S. buyers, are in for continued failure and losses.

GOING BACK TO SCHOOL

Global markets and global competition will be the future of marketing services for consultants into the twenty-first century. Depending on this area as a major source of income implies that consultants must be able to establish professional alliances, get responsible answers quickly for clients in a broad range of areas concerning multiple markets, and help clients establish both long-term and short-range trading agreements and partnerships. In larger organizations and manufacturing environments, acquisitions and alliances are the order of the day, but they develop and are sealed at an ever-faster pace. Woe to the consultant who cannot keep up!

In turn, consultants who do not have significant expertise in these areas should think about going back to school before telling clients that they can be of help. Courses in international finance, international politics, languages, economics—even geography—may be the best way to ensure future success.

RECOMMENDED READINGS

"Are Europe's Companies Becoming More European?," *The Economist* (June 27, 1987).

Daltas, A., and P. McDonald, "Barricades to Strategic Marketing Thinking," *Planning Review* 15 (1) (Jan-Feb 1987).

Ghoshal, S., "Global Strategy: An Organizing Framework," *Strategic Management Journal* 8 (1987).

Kotler, P., L. Fahey, and S. Jatusripitak, *The New Competition: What Theory Z Didn't Tell You About—MARKETING* (Englewood Cliffs, N.J.: Prentice-Hall, 1985).

Pitzer, M. J., "Most U.S. Companies Are Innocents Abroad," *Business Week* (Nov. 16, 1987).

Stern, L. W., and F. D. Sturdivant, "Customer-Driven Distribution Systems," *Harvard Business Review* 65 (4) (July-Aug. 1987).

Takeuchi, H., and I. Nonaka, "The New New Product Development Game," *Harvard Business Review* 64 (1) (Jan.-Feb. 1986).

Wernerfelt, B., "The Relation between Market Share and Profitability," *Journal of Business Strategy* 6 (4) (Spring 1986).

"Why Goliath Can't Export," *The Economist* (July 11, 1987).

CHAPTER 9

NEW TECHNOLOGIES, OPERATIONS, AND SYSTEMS SUPPORT

DEFINING THE PROBLEM

The Housekeepers and their machine bureaucracies have given American business a taste for quick fixes and easily describable problems. Television, summary journalism, and stock analysts focused on quarterly earnings have so destroyed the national attention span that our clients' eyes glaze over whenever we discuss issues that can be addressed only with time, energy, and deep involvement. Such issues include organizational change, the modification of organizational values, strategic planning and investment, the long-term development of overseas markets, and management succession planning—in other words, many of the most important issues facing American business. This thirst for the quick fix explains, for example, why so many manufacturers have plunged like lemmings into total integration, robotics, and every other kind of automation that promises instant improvement—and why so many of those firms also eventually wake up with incredible organizational, financial, and technical "hangovers." And these are the "forward-thinking" firms that have at least attempted some level of change through the use of technology. Most of their competitors still are in various states of denial—hoping against odds that the government will come to their aid or fantasizing that global competition is just a passing fad.

In any case, technology, manufacturing, automation, and the like will be fertile fields for consultants to plow in the next decade. To provide consulting services in this area, the first step is to define what the issues are. Some of the most basic issues can be broken down as follows:

- Mechanistic management versus organic management,
- Mechanistic manufacturing versus organic manufacturing,
- Developing specific objectives for automation,

- Understanding the full impact of automation,
- Valuing and respecting patience as a part of the renewal process.

MANAGEMENT ISSUES

We have already looked at many issues involved in changing from mechanistic to organic concepts and values in management. This may be the time, however, for a brief review of some of the basic differences as they relate to manufacturing.

146

Mechanistic Management	Organic Management
Workers assumed to be pay driven	Workers want challenging work
Traditional jobs	Self-design jobs and team approach
Pyramidal structure, many layers	Organization flat with few layers and employees close to the customer
Workers suspect, minimal investment in training and development	Worker input sought with heavy investment in training and development
Hire and fire based on economy	Fewer but more permanent jobs
Pay is based on job description	Gain sharing and multiple fringes
Labor and management enemies	Labor and management partners
Product driven, customer takes what's offered	Customer driven, customer can change production output

This may seem ancient history now, especially to consultants who have kept up with the literature or who have had the challenge and pleasure of working with clients striving for renewal. We must remember, however, that machine bureaucracy concepts were still being taught in the early 1970s and that most executives educated around that time or earlier didn't go on to master's level degrees. Yet these managers are now reaching the peak of their business careers! Some have probably learned something about the new innovative, organic approaches to management if they have been successful at a *Fortune* 500 company, where there often is heavy commitment to management development and a constant influx of newly minted M.B.A.s. But there are thousands of other managers in this age group who remain in small or family-owned and managed firms and who have not gotten the word about the values and concepts of rebirth and renewal as much as consultants would like to believe.

MANUFACTURING ISSUES

The basic change from mechanistic to organic management has its correlate in the evolutionary—or revolutionary—change from mechanistic to organic manufacturing. This area is where the real stress of global competition is found and the changes often have been the deepest.

147

Mechanistic Manufacturing	Organic (Flexible) Manufacturing
Long-term capital investments leading to mass production	Short-term investments, outsourcing, or leasing
Long production runs based on economies of scale	Basic products with multiple options for customer interface with system
Single-use products	Multiple-use and multiple markets and products
Quality has a price tradeoff	Quality is the solution to all issues
Single-source suppliers	Multiple suppliers of same parts
Large inventories (just in case)	Negligible inventories (just in time)
Unskilled, unionized labor	Highly skilled, nonunion labor
Industrial engineers are king	Plant managers are king
Capital-oriented environment	People-oriented environment

The extent of these differences would seem to explain, clearly, why American manufacturers in mature and declining industries are hard pressed to keep up with their global competitors, especially the Japanese. Professor Martin Starr at Columbia University has performed major research throughout the

United States and Japan to understand what effect, if any, Japanese management ("2001 manufacturing") has on a firm. He interviewed managers at some 250 U.S.-based manufacturing firms owned by Japanese companies—some very small, with less than a dozen employees, others as large as the Honda plant in Tennessee. Professor Starr then compared the performance of these companies to their Japanese parent firms and to their U.S.-owned competitors. In more than 85 percent of the firms he analyzed, Starr found that, even with just a few senior Japanese people speaking fluent English and teaching Japanese (2001) manufacturing techniques, the U.S.-based Japanese-owned firms were performing at about 90 percent of the productivity and efficiency levels of their parent Japanese firms and at about three to four times the efficiency of their U.S.-owned rivals. This may explain why, in 1988, Honda-USA began exporting some of its cars to Japan! In support of Starr's findings, productivity and manufacturing experts alike have learned over the past ten years that it is not the *national* culture—Japanese or American or European—but the *corporate* culture that makes the difference. Most Japanese are behaviorally indistinguishable from Americans in the work place or with friends or family; and even in Japan itself, not all companies are equally well managed or successful. But there are some Japanese companies that distinguish themselves from all others in their commitment: first, to their workers; second, to their customers; and third, to the quality of their products and the management of their production costs. In the United States we have come to recognize them as Minolta, Mitsubishi, Canon, Casio, Honda, Toyota, and Nissan Motors. But researchers also bring back the news that for every one of these incredibly well-run companies in Japan, there are hundreds that are poorly managed. Here in the United States we are no different. Companies such as Omark Industries, Hewlett-Packard, Nucor Steel, Apple Computer, 3M, and many more are exceptionally well managed and have the same fierce dedication to their employees and to quality as their Japanese counterparts.

THE NEED FOR SPECIFIC OBJECTIVES

In the quest for instant gratification and a 2001 factory, many a CEO has tried to order a whole, fully integrated manufacturing system all at once—automatic assembly, automatic tool changing, machine inspection, automated materials handling, computer-aided design (CAD), computer-numerical control (CNC), and so on. But when a $25 million company spends the $5 to $6 million in capital expenditure that this kind of manufacturing system will cost, it means the CEO is betting the farm! Before a client goes off on such a tear, there are dozens of questions that ought to be generated by a conscientious consultant asked to help with such a decision. What in the world would this CEO do with such a toy? Would he spend that kind of money if he owned the company and it was all coming directly out of his own pocket? What are the long-range objectives of so total a conversion, so immense an investment? Are the firm's competitors that committed? To whom is the firm going to sell the quadrupled output to pay for all of this? Are the new tolerances purchased with such quality control (QC) limits really needed for this business and the firm's current or projected customers? Has the firm analyzed its current operations thoroughly and made all of the improvements possible before committing to a program of automation?

SIMPLISTIC APPROACHES TO COMPLEX PROBLEMS

As we have seen again and again, simplistic approaches and hastily implemented solutions to enormously complex problems just do not work. Often they lead to the creation of many more problems than they solve. This axiom is nowhere more true than when managers and executives assume that the impact of automation or robotics in a formerly nonautomated shop will be restricted principally to those workers replaced by the automation. I do not believe a dairy cow thinks this linearly! Yet hundreds of manufacturing managers, reared on mechanistic manufacturing concepts, decided that perhaps they should upgrade and automate. Because of their "genetic imprinting" they tend to make decisions based on the following assumptions:

- Automated processes, because they are mechanical and computer controlled, can be snapped-on in place and begin working almost immediately.
- Because of automation, the real gains are to be had through laying off the most expensive labor and leaving in place just a few "button pushers" at entry grades.
- The automated part of the company or plant is a discreet part of the organization, and what happens there will have little impact on how the rest of the plant operates until those other areas are automated.
- Automation will improve quality instantly.

Each of these beliefs is a myth in its own right and a ferocious trap waiting to swallow up another innocent neophyte in plant conversion. Automated processes and robotic elements are finely tuned and often have narrow tolerances. They must be custom-developed depending on the item being manufactured, the function to be automated, the physical layout of the line, and so forth. Implementation usually takes months, moving a step at a time, an element at a time. Furthermore, some of the more sophisticated elements may take additional months of fine-tuning to get CAM-based systems to where they actually are able to outperform the humans they replaced.

Because these robotic elements and other automated functions of production are so sophisticated, they require "rocket scientists" to repair them when they malfunction. Therefore, contrary to popular belief, it is not the most expensive workers who are obsolesced by automation, but the least trained and least expensive. The best trained, brightest, and highest paid are the only ones able to cope with the further training needed to understand how to maximize the usefulness of the automation and service it when it goes down. You can imagine the frustration, then, of managers in the aerospace industry who find their high school "graduate" hires functionally illiterate and first-line supervisors unable to operate simple hand-held calculators.

■ CASE IN POINT   151
The greatest training expense at TRW's plants in Southern California is for training entry-level nonexempt staff in basic reading and writing skills!

Further, the idea that automation in one part of the plant or at one end of the line can somehow be isolated from everything else in the company is naive at best. Because automated processes often have narrower tolerances, input systems must be monitored more closely than before. Even suppliers may be affected with respect to the quality standards of the parts or raw materials they provide. As the quality of the automated output improves, other, follow-on steps in the manufacturing process from finishing to packaging must also improve. Although automated manufacturing processes may directly affect only one part of the plant, they can and must indirectly affect everyone and everything in the company if it is to realize a return on its investment.

The idea that automation and especially robotics will bring an instant improvement in quality is also a dangerous myth. In fact, nothing could be further from the truth. As automation and robotics allow manufacturers to break away from the long, inflexible Experience Curve runs developed for machine bureau-cracy environments, the resulting organic production lines, attuned to customer needs, tend to break up into shorter, dis-crete production lines whose quality criteria change constantly. Such a system is simply not envisioned by the Taylor school of manufacturing management—the system that reigned for sev-enty-five years in this country and that still drives many mature manufacturing lines. As a result, even the most advanced op-erations do not have the kind of production and control systems that can accommodate the short runs and client-driven systems of twenty-first century organic manufacturing. About the closest thing to what may be needed are the self-design work groups as defined by Tom Cummings and his colleagues at USC.

152

"BALLOON-BREAKING" AND THE "BONZO-BANANA" CULTURE

Consultants working with clients interested in introducing or ex-panding automation in their factories and plants must test the client's assumptions about what the automation is going to ac-complish before going into any specifics. In those cases where unrealistic or even foolish criteria have been established, the consultant must help bring the client back to reality. Such "bal-loon-breaking" is particularly necessary in the type of corporate culture I like to call *Bonzo-Banana!* (in reference to the early space flights with chimpanzee passengers). Such cultures are characterized by a mentality wherein management expects in-stant technological gratification at the push of a button.

In "Bonzo-Banana" cultures, if nothing happens when managers push the button, their interest wanes quickly.

Obviously, this is the worst possible corporate environment in which to develop or introduce new automation because the discipline required to develop new systems just isn't a part of the culture. It is a consultant's responsibility to counsel such organizations as to the limits of their systems development capabilities imposed by the lack of self-discipline in their corporate culture. On the other hand, in cases where the consultant has been brought in after the fact to resolve the problems resulting from too many burst balloons, it may be necessary to take the client back to square one and reevaluate why automation was acquired and what the objectives are in both the short and long term.

■CASE IN POINT

Over the years IBM has found that customers tend to go through three emotional states when introducing new systems: euphoria—it works!; depression—it doesn't do everything we hoped for; and studied optimism—it still is a fine, flexible system. Clients need a great deal of empathy and assistance through all three phases.

Another role the consultant plays is helping the client address the implementation steps, planning, and timing that must accompany the successful introduction of automation. Jeffrey Liker of the University of Michigan and his colleagues found that clients have basically two choices: first introducing the technical systems, and then dealing with the organizational issues; or, first introducing the organizational changes, and then dealing with the technical systems. Liker found that there are pros and cons to each path. The first approach develops from the premise that, if the technology is developed first, the organizational impacts can be dealt with gradually as the automation comes on line stage by stage. This way, there should be a minimum of disruption and smoother integration in the organization around those areas where the technology is installed.

The latter position was developed from experiences at John Deere, Inc. in the introduction of their large-scale flexible manufacturing systems, together with research done on a number of large public libraries introducing new technological systems. It all seems to support the argument that it is better to deal first with organizational and sociological issues, so that when the technology is introduced, employees will be understanding and supportive of what is occurring and not resist it. These sociological issues cannot be minimized. They include not only the obvious issue of worker resistance to the threat of lost jobs, but the enormous changes wrought by automation to the jobs which remain. Many workers find that their old jobs have been changed completely. That may sound exciting to us, but it can be terrifying to a blue-collar worker or a supervisor who has been doing virtually the same things for ten or fifteen years. It is equally disruptive when automation brings downsizing and layoffs, when it demands even finer tolerances in the product and the systems, or when workers are asked to develop new working relationships with one another. Such developments can be even more traumatic than reorganizing for growth.

154

HOW MUCH AUTOMATION, ANYWAY?

Richard Schonberger is president of Schonberger & Associates in Seattle, Washington, a firm that specializes in manufacturing management assistance. After dealing with hundreds of manufacturers who all want to mortgage the farm to automate their firms, Schonberger has learned to make his clients question just how much automation their firms need. He contends that because of the constraints placed on manufacturers by mechanistic management approaches, often you can make a great deal of basic improvement before introducing any automation at all. This approach, in turn, is based on the client's ability to continually modify, customize, and simplify equipment as quality standards and customer needs change. Consultants wanting to build practices in this area would be wise, then, to learn how to ask the right questions, especially, "Why automate now? Have you already done everything possible to maximize productivity with your existing equipment and system?"

TECHNOLOGY TRAINING—THE NEXT GREAT MARKET

About the year 1970, Arthur Andersen senior management met to map out the future of the firm in the management consulting field. At that time, the firm made what seemed to be a highly risky decision to concentrate exclusively in information systems support at the expense of all other consulting markets—from strategy to marketing, organization design, and executive search. We all know that the gamble paid off and AA went on to become the largest consulting firm in the world. Today, its principal rivals are not other consulting firms or Big-8 audit firms as much as large companies in the information systems and technology field such as IBM and EDS. In the summer of 1987, AA senior management had another such far-reaching conference to map out the next fifteen years of its consulting practice. Obviously, much of what they decided was proprietary, but three momentous decisions for the firm and the industry have become public knowledge.

The first decision is that the management services or consulting division of the firm will no longer report to the audit division but will break off into a parallel and altogether separate organization. The rationale for this is straightforward. Because their competition is not the other Big-8 audit firms, and because they would like to attract the "best and the brightest" to consult in the field of technology, the consulting division must be able to develop its own compensation structure more in line with its real competitors rather than the audit division or the other Big-8 firms.

They also decided to add two major areas—Strategic Services and Education Consulting—within the general area of systems technology, a decision that shows even more foresight. AA breaks the field of Education Consulting down into three parts: organization change, knowledge transfer, and technology assimilation (robotics, AI, and CAD/CAM). It is clear from its decision that Arthur Andersen recognizes that the full range of consultant services needed by the industry goes beyond the design and development of specific systems. To ignore the equally important need for education and the facilitation of change still smacks of mechanistic management. Indeed, the latest surveys of white-collar productivity in the United States, developed by the merchant banking firm of Morgan Stanley in New York, show that in 1986 overall U.S. productivity improved somewhat, but white-collar productivity declined 6 percent. In other words, systems and technology for their own sake cannot help resolve wider problems.

What AA has committed itself to, and what this chapter tries to clarify, is the need for consultants to look beyond clients' demands to automate or create and install a system.

Historically, we have tended to think of systems as being comprised of people, processes, and technology, yet we have concentrated our efforts on the processes and the technology, often overlooking the people.

In the future, consultants must attune themselves to their clients' needs as far as modifying their organizations to accommodate new technologies and processes. If automation and technology is to improve productivity and allow this nation to remain competitive in manufacturing markets, there must be a formal, thorough transfer of knowledge about systems and technology from the technicians to the managers and employees.

Arthur Andersen's new Education Consulting organization holds great promise for the firm and for our industry. The firm estimates that through 1995 the market for technology assimilation could be as large as $15 billion, the market for knowledge transfer between $7 and $20 billion, and that for organizational change consulting between $4 and $6 billion. That's a rough spread of $15 to $40 billion in new consulting markets that are only now emerging. With such opportunities before all of us, it behooves consultants to familiarize themselves with the issues developing in this area. Peat Marwick Main understands the potential and showed its commitment by sponsoring the Advanced Manufacturing Systems Exposition in Chicago in 1988 under the leadership of their Chicago partner, Bill Ainsworth. Peat is competing aggressively with AA in certain niches of what used to be its exclusive market.

ARTIFICIAL INTELLIGENCE—THE REAL 2001 SYSTEM

Artificial Intelligence is a field still in its infancy. It will be another decade before AI has widespread use in our society. Two of the leading experts, Roger Schank of Yale and Patrick Winston of MIT, have broken through the technological obfuscation surrounding AI to explain clearly what it is and what it now can do. Basically, they agree that AI is best used to recreate or "clone" information, especially technical information, about technology, finance, economics, management systems, the stockmarket, or whatever. This data can be developed into complex programs or "expert systems" with which a user can interact almost as with a human expert. For example, a stockbroker in

South Dakota might be able to turn his client over to an AI system based in the broker's New York office, a system that "contains" all the expert knowledge of the firm's best analysts. The client can ask questions and get advice from the AI system that the less-experienced broker in South Dakota could not hope to provide. It takes upward of five man-years to write such a program.

We can envision a vast array of such relationships and systems used in engineering consulting firms, financial services companies, medical seminars, schools, and, yes, even management consulting firms. We can even imagine a time in the not so distant future when McKinsey might open an office in Cheyenne, Wyoming. When someone drops by—which may happen no more than once a year—he or she can just slip a credit card in the slot and hook up to the New York office where AI systems have recorded all of the genius of all of the managers of the firm's past two generations of leadership!

For the moment, there still are only two ways AI can be used effectively: (1) small jobs with short-term payoffs, where the competency of the system can be tested and proven fairly easily, and (2) the megaprojects that attempt to capture the knowledge of the experts as exemplified in the illustration above. In all AI development, however, the systems are found to be fraught with error—human error—in the assumptions (and assumptions about assumptions) that comprise the expert knowledge and skill. The result may be fallacious reasoning or major gaps in logic.

Consultants wanting to develop business in this area need to do several things. First, they must identify those institutions near their base of operations—experimental labs, university research shops, and so forth—where new developments and applications are taking place in AI. The field is too new for either the basic concepts or the specific applications to be static. There will continue to be great change in this area for some time to come, and the consultants earning the reputation as the most knowledgeable will be the ones plugged into the technology leaders and their research, trials, and errors. Second, it will be necessary to identify which potential clients can utilize AI now and possibly into the future. Where is it applicable, how is it applicable, and what level of activity is required to pay back the enormous start-up and developmental costs? These are not difficult questions, but they tend to limit where AI is currently applicable.

EXCITING POSSIBILITIES

Between the $40 billion market potential of education consulting, the emergence of practical uses for Artificial Intelligence, and the manifold challenges posed by the development of global markets and competition, consultants have their plates full. Here again, however, the consultants who will do more than just survive—the ones who will lead the industry into the next century—will be those able to help their clients with a broad array of dynamic services and organic approaches. They include

- Defining the extent of automation required,
- Maximizing extant production facilities and equipment,
- Planning for the implementation of new technology by stressing sociological impacts and organic programs,
- Going beyond automation implementation to deal with technology transfer, knowledge assimilation, and organizational change,
- Identifying potential uses for artificial intelligence systems,
- Helping clients cope with the effects of improved productivity and the downsizing that will result from all of the above.

Consultants well versed in automation, robots, and state-of-the-art technologies can do more to assist U.S. industry in its quest for renewal in this one field alone than in any other area of endeavor. It will be in this arena in the next decade that American businesses will be able to regain price and quality leadership across a wide range of products and markets. Consultants and consulting firms able to lead the way for clients through sensitive management training and careful applications analyses will be among the principal winners.

RECOMMENDED READINGS

160

Buffa, E., *Meeting the Competitive Challenge: Manufacturing Strategies for U.S. Companies* (Homewood, Ill: Irwin, 1984).

Cohen, S. S. ,and J. Zysman, "Why Manufacturing Matters: The Myth of the Post-Industrial Economy," *California Management Review* 29 (3) (Spring 1987).

Ernst, R. G., "How to Streamline Operations," *Journal of Business Strategy* 8 (2) (Fall 1987).

Ferdows, Kasra, and Wickham Skinner, "The Sweeping Revolution in Manufacturing," *Journal of Business Strategy* 8 (2) (Fall 1987).

Hoerr, J., et al., "Management Discovers the Human Side of Automation: A Special Report," *Business Week* (Sept. 1986).

Hutchinson, D., *Quality Circles Handbook* (New York: Nicholas, 1985).

Liker, J. K., et al., "Changing Everything All at Once: Work Life and Technological Change," *Sloan Management Review* 28 (4) (Summer 1987).

Port, Otis, "The Push for Quality: A Special Report," *Business Week* (June 8, 1987).

Scheil, B., "Thinking about Artificial Intelligence," *Harvard Business Review* 65 (4) (July-Aug. 1987).

Schonberger, Richard J., "Frugal Manufacturing," *Harvard Business Review* 65 (5) (Sept.-Oct. 1987).

Simon, R., "The Morning After: A Science and Technology Feature," *Forbes* (Oct. 19, 1987).

Sink, D. S., *Productivity Management: Measurement and Evaluation, Control and Improvement* (New York: Wiley, 1985).

Smith, M. A., "Improving Product Quality in American Industry," *Academy of Management's Executive* 1 (3) (Aug. 1987).

Tierno, D. A., "Growth Strategies for Consulting in the Next Decade," *Sloan Management Review* 27 (2) (Winter 1986).

Walton, R. E., and G. I. Susman, "People Policies for the New Machines," *Harvard Business Review* 65 (2) (March-April 1987).

Witney, J. O., "Turnaround Management Every Day," *Harvard Business Review* 65 (5) (Sept.-Oct. 1987).

TODAY'S LESSONS AND TOMORROW'S CONSULTANTS

HELPING THE HUMAN PROCESS

When I consider how many of the technologies and industries thriving today didn't exist just five years ago, and think of the unforetold technologies yet to be developed and the industries in turn to be built off them, I also wonder what management consultants will be doing twenty-five, fifty, or a hundred years from now. The probable answer is very much what we do today! Bob Atteyah of McKinsey & Company—alluding to the famous joke that consultants just borrow their clients' watches to tell them the time—freely admits that some of his best consulting has indeed involved taking ideas that already exist within client organizations, helping bring them to the surface so they can be used, and thus creating permanent, positive change. I myself define consulting as the act of creatively helping the human process. Organizations don't get themselves into trouble, people do. Organizations don't stifle innovation, mechanistic people do. Organizations don't squander profits, poorly focused people do. On the other hand, organizations have no sense of the future, no vision, no urge to test their true mettle, but people do. Consultants deal with people—all kinds of people in all kinds of situations. We are idea-generators and father-confessors, agents of change, and systems psychiatrists. But whatever we do, it always involves people. I cannot envision people or their basic emotions changing any more in the next hundred years than they have changed in the last three thousand.

Harry Levinson, the great managerial psychologist from the Harvard Medical School, likes to point out that Moses was the first consultant. Extrapolating from the Bible, Levinson argues that Moses, a stranger, took the Israelites from their painful yet familiar (mechanistic) bondage under the Egyptians. Some of his followers resisted this change, while others still sought structured leadership in the desert. Moses recognized that some people took a long view and were willing to sacrifice, while others demanded immediate gratification. It was a difficult job for Moses, one in which the solution to the problem demanded that the Israelites take on a new kind of bondage—the bondage of voluntary laws, social responsibilities, and a code for living. And Moses recognized that you can't wash away the dirt of centuries from former slaves. (Nor can you sell third wave solutions to managers with a lifetime built on second wave concepts.) To allow the transition to take effect, Moses used a participatory or process approach, but according to Levinson's analogy, Moses argued with his people at least as much as he argued with God. He was generally more successful with God!

There always will be small, family-owned and -managed companies trying to reinvent the wheel at an ungodly cost. There always will be powerful *Fortune* 1,000 executives who have insatiable appetites for ever-larger machine bureaucracies and who ignore the internal chaos and inefficiencies of these megaorganizations. Most important, there always will be small and medium-sized companies starting to grow, yet unable to afford the cost of full-time experts to manage their growth successfully. Burt Nanus, a futurist at the University of Southern California and a consultant to a number of companies on the *Fortune* list, notes that over the past twenty years, "*Fortune* 1,000 employment has remained quite stable and is likely to remain so for the next twenty years due to productivity improvements and the introduction of additional automation." It is the smaller firms in this country, he notes, that will see a growth in their employment and the corresponding need for organization design, new forms of compensation, and creative, organic planning and marketing.

CONSULTING TO SMALL BUSINESSES

With the majority of all consultants working "solo" or for smaller practices, many deal with businesses employing fewer than fifty or one hundred employees. This aspect of our profession has been researched considerably over the past few years. Many of the findings are self-explanatory or even obvious, but all are important, with enormous implications for consultants who wish to be successful in this market. Some of these findings include the following:

- Small company management often has no clear vision of where it wants to take the company, or if it does have a vision, no concept about how to achieve the goals and objectives developed.
- Smaller firms seldom have useful information systems. The financials are often kept on a quarterly or semi-annual basis by outside accountants and bookkeepers, and operations generally are managed by a seat-of-the pants approach. Few performance standards exist.
- The entrepreneurs who start new companies are frequently driven by their own creativity and talent, and they often lose interest in the administrative or organizational details required to manage their efforts after a certain level of success.
- Small companies cannot relate to the *Fortune* 1,000 company models or case studies often used by sophisticated consultants. They may need a content approach that teaches management skills as much as they need anything.
- There has been very little developed in the way of case materials or articles on small businesses, their problems, and their relationships with consultants. Almost all of the developmental materials constructed to date focus on larger companies and their issues.
- Small companies need more help to survive and grow than larger firms that have already passed certain developmental stages in their corporate lives, yet because they are small, they cannot afford normal consultant fees. Alternative compensation schemes must be negotiated if the consultant-client relationship is to take hold and grow.

All of the above makes consulting to small companies distinctively different from consulting to the *Fortune* 1,000. Small company owners and managers tend to be less trustful of the mechanistic approach used by consultants in large, mature organizations. These managers are the true Tank Commanders. They expect any consultants they engage to roll up their sleeves and share a part of the work load. In larger firms, conversely, consultants are rarely called on to be surrogate managers anymore. Some less sophisticated small company managers, unfamiliar with the new breed of academic independent, distrust highly educated M.B.A.s and Ph.D.s and perceive them as being too theoretical, inexperienced in the real world, and unable to practice what they preach. Larger firms, on the other hand, hire consultants precisely for the sophistication of their studies and knowledge. Finally, where larger firms usually hire consultants for their narrow expertise in a particular area—compensation, organization design, strategy development, and so forth—smaller firms are looking for consultants with a broad range of experience, generalists rather than specialists, who can be like the staff in these firms, involved in a wide range of functions.

Consultants should understand, in other words, that small business consulting is a unique area of the profession. Clients require special perspectives, experience, and sensitivity on the part of the consultant if the relationship is to be successful and the consultant accepted in the organization. Further, many of the mechanistic skills and expertise prized by large, mature organizations have little value to these smaller, organic enterprises, which tend to trust and value different skills. Small, young businesses in growth stages may have fuzzy goals and little practical information with which consultants can work to identify root causes of organizational problems or devise solutions. There is even a dearth of literature or case studies on small companies to aid consultants, even those attempting to

166

perform action research. As a result, consultants who have the opportunity to provide services to this segment of the market must proceed with caution and sensitivity to issues that can undermine their consulting efforts.

CONSULTING TO FAMILY BUSINESSES

The family-controlled enterprise also has unique issues, needs, and problems, some of them having to do with size, and some having to do with ownership. Such companies typically have strategic problems with their organizational values, and they often lack a clear mission statement. They hold a rich potential for consulting opportunities and challenges—and dangerous traps for the inexperienced consultant.

167

Whenever anyone mentions "family-owned businesses," whether in an M.B.A. class or at a cocktail party, most listeners think of "mom and pop" stores or the neighborhood dry cleaners. But if the term is taken to mean "businesses controlled substantially, but not necessarily completely, by one family or one person," one can generate a striking statistic.

By this definition, 85 percent of all businesses in the United States, estimated to generate as much as 50 percent of the gross national product, are "family-owned."

Included on this list, of course, are Levi Strauss, Coors Breweries, Hallmark Cards, and dozens of family empires such as those controlled by the Hunts in Texas, or Lesley Wexner (The Limited). Of the *Fortune* 500, approximately 175 companies are family controlled. Just perusing the *Forbes* annual list of "The Wealthiest 400 Families in America" is an education in the role of the family in American business.

But family-controlled firms are tough clients. Most consultants, even experienced ones, get caught in two critical contradictions unique to family controlled firms. The first is the conflict between the pragmatic, here and now needs of the firm versus the longer-range emotional needs of the family members. The second conflict is between the different overlapping spheres of influence—family members, other owners, managers, and employees—all of which are often in conflict with one another for resources. John Davis of USC's School of Business Administration is preeminent in this area of consulting and management research. He has developed a model, which appears below:

168

DAVIS'S FAMILY BUSINESS SYSTEMS CONCEPT

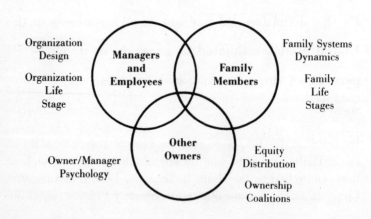

Davis's research and long-standing consulting practice with family-owned businesses have taught him that an individual associated with such an enterprise can be found in one, two, or all three of these circles. Perhaps the most critical aspect of the model is that of ownership, both family and otherwise. In most family-controlled businesses it is difficult for a consultant to learn the details of ownership, even when the family has called the consultant in to advise on some aspect of the firm. This secrecy is not as much a rational concern that some confidential data might be shared with other outsiders or even employees or competitors as it is an emotional reluctance to allow the consultant, an outsider, access to the family's personal financial data and bank accounts. No matter how hard the consultant may reassure the family client, he or she will always be suspect.

Another highly sensitive area is that of equity distribution between family owners and nonfamily owners. In such situations, who gets what is an issue as old as time itself, and many a novel has been written about a family with majority ownership trying to wrestle the remaining control from nonfamily members or not being willing to share earnings fairly. When nonfamily ownership is involved, how the family and nonfamily forces join together in the ownership coalition can be a major issue. Consultants must realize that, because family members are usually discreet and secretive with outsiders, it is often a crisis in ownership that prompts the engagement of an outside consultant in the first place.

Consultants also must be particularly sensitive to the family structure itself. Which generation represents ownership? Which generation represents present and future management? What are the variant needs of each generation? Where are they mutually supportive or in conflict? A classic situation occurs when the younger generation in management wants to use family assets to expand the company but the older generation wants to preserve family assets and assure its security in retirement. An equally devastating problem is the conflict between an older generation committed to an old particular paradigm of management and a younger generation, often with freshly won M.B.A.s, wanting to use third wave management values and approaches. The classic discussion between these generations goes like this: One side asks, "How can you want to change things? It's the way we've always managed and there would be no company today if we hadn't done it this way!" The other side counters, "It might have worked in your generation, Mom and Dad, but if you keep doing things the same old way, there will be no company for our generation to manage!"

■ CASE IN POINT

170

Although two sons were managing a family-controlled bank in South Texas under their father's leadership in his role as chairman, the brightest sibling in the family was the daughter, who had gone off and earned an M.B.A. at a good school. Because money and the business were "men's work," however, her ideas and suggestions about managing the bank were almost totally ignored, even after the bank ran into serious problems and sought outside expertise. The business came very close to failing before the males of the family could bring themselves to accept guidance from "Daddy's little girl."

The nature of family relationships can cause a number of problems that affect the business. Sometimes powerful family members who are retired from the business or not involved in it at all—such as the founder's widow—still assume, because of their family role, that they also have an equally powerful voice in company affairs. Another example of family power is the father who plans and arranges for the eldest son to be the next president and CEO, based solely on the ancient rights of the first born, while a more competent daughter or younger son is relegated to a minor role or not encouraged to enter the family business at all.

Finally, there is the third aspect of Davis's model—management and employees. In family-owned firms, nonfamily members can traditionally aspire only to certain management levels; members of the family will be the executive vice president, the president, and the CEO. Familiar examples abound of the young son with little practical experience leapfrogging over more competent managers to attain a vice presidency solely because of his family ties. Other problems in this area include the amount the family may choose to spend or not spend on employee fringe benefits, salaries, and management perquisites and the classic issue of powerful family members who deal directly with anyone in the firm, ignoring completely the organization structure or lines of authority and responsibility. Although some of this behavior is becoming a thing of the past, especially in very large family-controlled firms such as Ford, in smaller family-owned firms, such practices still continue today. As a result, talented workers and managers tend to leave as fast as they can be found; and family firms that practice such tribal discrimination tend to be left with less than stellar talent and a predominance of employees who have little aspiration or hope of promotion much beyond their current status. Is it any wonder, then, that these firms must eventually turn to outside consultants?

171

Consultants dealing with these family-controlled firms must understand all three aspects of the Davis model if they are to help the firm come to grips with its problems and implement positive change. Kelin Gersick of the California School of Professional Psychology adds a further dimension to the complexities of dealing with family firms. He points out the conflict existing between the traditional, long-term approach used by psychologists and therapists to counsel family members with respect to family crises versus the short-term, here-and-now approach used by business consultants to turn ailing firms around. When the firm is a family enterprise, these two methods of therapy create yet another contradiction. Consultants working with troubled family-controlled enterprises must have great sensitivity to the longer-term therapeutic approaches necessary to heal family wounds in addition to the short-term tactics used to improve sales, profits, or other measures of performance.

EVERYTHING HAS A FIVE-YEAR OBSOLESCENCE—INCLUDING US

Given these problems of the small or family-owned business, and all the threatening new strategic concerns that, as we have seen throughout this book, are currently afflicting the *Fortune* 1,000, there has never been as much business available to management consultants. But there is a price to be paid for this overabundance of clientele. The busier we are, the less current our services. The more we have to do, the more we tend to do the same thing. The more we do the same thing, the more apt it is to be out-of-date and ineffective. Consultants need to perform R&D as much as their clients. One way to do this is to periodically return to academia, to read, to reflect, to perform solid research in areas of interest, and to teach. By doing so, we learn what the latest thinking is and how it may be applicable to our clients. We rejuvenate our professional disciplines, discover new ideas and methods of doing things, and get rid of the biases that may have accumulated in the previous five years—biases about why things don't work and why people behave as they do, biases about labor, about management, about international issues—all the false logic and ill-perceived facts that build up like wax on a coffee table when you don't have enough time to read or be reflective.

My time invested at the University of Southern California has been priceless for me. Not only have I been continually challenged by bright, eager graduate students, but I also have had the opportunity to read more than ever and to perform some meaningful action research in my chosen industry, financial services. With Professor Sukhen Dey of Indiana University, I performed seminal market research on upscale customer preferences and attitudes that later was not only confirmed by further research performed with other banks but also was used as background by the Senate Banking and Finance Committee to draft new legislation. Ari Ginsberg of NYU's Graduate School of Business Administration and I performed groundbreaking work on Japanese banking in the United States and discovered that its performance has been much more problematic than the raw statistics indicate. And I have had the opportunity to collaborate and write on a broad range of subjects: about high-performance banking organizations with Tom Cummings and electronic offshore clerical sweat shops with Mary Ann Von Glinow, also of USC.

173

None of this puts me in the $10,000-a-day league, but it does allow me to think more broadly about issues and how they affect my clients. Going back to school periodically is, I think, a responsibility to ourselves and to our clients that we all hold as professionals. Most of us live or work near enough to a college or business school that we can explore such opportunities. Certainly, my years in academia cut into the hours available for consulting, but I believe it all will come back to me in the long term. There is no question that it will extend my usefulness for a few more years.

ADMINISTRATIVE SPACE STATIONS

At the same time, the exponential curve of change is remorseless. Even for the consultant who is state-of-the-art it is difficult at times to imagine what's next. Apple Computer is working on an interface between compact laser discs (CLDs) and its newest personal computers whereby a user will be able to boot up a four-inch disc containing the entire Encyclopedia Britannica for referencing. Cellular telephones have already shrunk to small hand-held sets priced for anyone with a credit card. As the new, higher-temperature superconductors are developed, computer power will explode while size will shrink even further. It is quite possible to imagine a lap top Apple II with a built-in laser printer within the next five years and an IBM AT portable the size of a large book within the decade.

Ultraflexible, high-impact epoxies and resins are transforming the newest-generation experimental aircraft to "all plastic," and those successes will carry over assuredly to the automotive field, so that by 2001 there will be little if any aluminum or steel used in the construction of planes, trains, or cars. Not only will this allow for higher speeds but also far greater fuel economy. Yet what are the implications for those of us with steel or aluminum companies as clients today? Kenichi Ohmae, Mc-Kinsey's consultant to Japan, notes that, although steel was the king of industries and drove entire economies for over 100 years, today electronics has taken over as the most powerful, fastest-growing, and richest industry. For example, whereas the value of all the circuits, chips, and electronic gadgetry in autos was barely 10 percent of a car's worth a few years ago, it is now as much as 30 percent of the total value of some cars today! Could it be that with the development of the new resins and improved polymers, plastics will become the industrial king of the next century?

Global competition among manufacturers and service companies has become so intense it is forcing all manner of innovation. For example, many *Fortune* 1,000 companies are now bundling up their daily paperwork, flying it overseas to Trinidad, or even mainland China, where it is microencoded by

174

workers paid as little as $1 a day. The finished tapes then are transmitted via satellite back to the United States with millions saved annually in clerical costs. Some pundits foresee this trend growing at an accelerated pace so that by the year 2001, half the *Fortune* 1,000 firms will be using some form of offshore administrative process to reduce salary expenses here in America. At the same time, what are the implications for entry-level and clerical positions in the United States over the next decade if this offshore trend continues? Will an entire generation of high school graduates be disenfranchised? On the other hand, if competitors are already using such systems, how can our existing clients avail themselves of these cost savings?

Although the trend to move production offshore may have troubling implications, here again we find a contradiction. Peter Drucker, in some of his latest writings, sees the organic enterprise of the 1990s and beyond as organized in small, functional units similar to the German management concept of *Gruppe*, where each decentralized unit has its own management. A data management unit could be offshore or across the country. Not only does this allow for flatter organizations across the total enterprise, but it permits more people an opportunity to test their managerial mettle and allows firms in renewal to develop more senior executives than the old machine bureaucracies ever did without a formal middle-management structure.

PREVENTING CLASSIC ERRORS

One of the basic and eternal roles of consultants that certainly will continue into the next century despite all this new technology and space-age logistics is helping clients avoid the classic management errors of past decades. Craig Apregan of Arthur Andersen talks in terms of client mismanagement models. It is clever way to generalize poor approaches to problem solving, and each of us could probably make up a few models of our own. Here are some of Craig's:

- *Slot Machine Management:* When managers lose hope they often enter a "Valley of Despair." In the valley, it appears that the only way out is to be extremely decisive, so they start making a lot of decisions quickly, as if loading nickels in a one-armed bandit, but they seldom line up three cherries, and these frantic efforts only make things worse.
- *Freudian Hydraulics:* As people's normal impatience gets worse and worse, it can become a powerful psychological force that makes people absolutely unable to wait. So they try to make something—anything—happen, and push unrealistically hard until it does. Such approaches take a heavy toll.

One of my own favorites is

- *The Charge of the Light Brigade:* This is management's propensity to keep right on doing whatever is running the firm into the ground simply because management has so much invested in the existing system of values and tenets that it cannot face the enormity of its error. This is an ego trap of immense proportions.

Of course one of *the* classic errors is to panic under crisis, and crisis management is one of the strongest growth sectors of consulting. At a recent annual meeting of the Academy of Management, Charley Mathews presented his analogy of crisis consulting to *The Wizard of Oz.* There are four distinct parts to Charley's crisis management: *the Crisis, the Journey, the Encounter* (with an authority figure), and *the Task.* In *The Wizard of Oz*, the Crisis is Dorothy's being swept up in the cyclone, the Tin Man's lack of a heart (to have compassion), the Lion's lack of courage (to face reality), and the Straw Man's lack of intellect (to compete). The Journey, of course, is the Yellow Brick Road (in real life it is the trip to Lourdes, the trek to Mecca) that leads to an authority figure who will solve the crisis. In business the journey may be a retreat to a wilderness resort by senior management to seek solutions or a search nationwide for the most capable management consulting firm to deal with the crisis at hand.

The Encounter with an authority figure describes Dorothy's meeting with the wizard. In real life, Mathews tells us, desperate people tend to see in authority figures what they hope and want to see. Consultants who deal in crisis management are particularly careful about what they say and how they say it because the client can misunderstand or attach too much importance to an idle comment.

Finally, there is the Task. It is meant to unfreeze and mobilize, to instill self-confidence and bind the group together. Dorothy and her friends found it fighting the Monkey People. Crisis consultants often use tasks as simple as data gathering to get a client operating again.

Most important is to understand the anxiety that precipitates crises in the first place. There would appear to be three principal forms of such anxiety. *Environmental overstimulation* can be brought on by anything from a successful Red Queen gambit by the competition to the curve of technological change and its impact on a particular process or industry. To deal with it, consultants must provide clear vision that can help clients regain their self-confidence. *Cognitive incongruity* is a reaction people may have to totally unexpected behavior that is in complete conflict with established values—such as the massive layoffs at AT&T or Kodak's closing of its Rochester developing lab. Here, role modeling and transformational leadership roles are called for. *Response unavailability* simply means that the client tried some particular mode of action but just couldn't deliver and so panic set in. Here, the consultant should help the client devise an action plan of small, attainable steps to get the client moving again.

AUTOMATION MEANS FEWER EXPERTS

Our clients need not more experts but more leaders and team players. Just as televisions isolated family members in the 1950s and 1960s, so also personal computers in the home are isolating family members even more so in the 1980s and 1990s. The same phenomenon is occurring in the work place. Workers have a relationship with a screen and the data on it, but how many have solid relationships with the employee who sits next to them? America has always been a very diversified society; but with productivity methods such as computer-based cottage industries serving larger organizations out of isolated homes and offices, employees are becoming less able to relate to a company's goals or to share something as basic as departmental-level motivations. The one-floor conglomerate façade supported by unattached cells of administrators physically shotgunned across the country is too fragmented to stick together for very long. There is too much isolation and not enough communality of purpose. I think it is very disturbing. And I am not alone in such concerns.

Michael Marcory, a Harvard researcher, notes that the impact of women in dual-worker families has been the most intensely researched topic of the past few years. Some of the findings are that, in families where the woman's income is greater or equal to the man's, the male is no longer the dominant authority. Each

178

person in such families makes his or her own authority. The implication of this for employers is worrisome, at best. Many children from such families are learning how to manage their parents—while learning that learning itself is necessary for survival.

Young people today don't trust their organizations any more than they trusted their busy parents to be there when they were needed.

This helps explain, among other things, why there is so much moonlighting and why so many employees have their own little enterprise going for them on the side these days. The result is cooler relationships overall, with less loyalty than ever. Even business schools are teaching students today how fickle the large machine bureaucracies have been as employers and urging them to be loyal first to their profession, whether accounting, law, finance, or human resource management. Consultants in the ensuing decades may have to spend an inordinate amount of time helping client organizations recognize that these attitudes are real and helping them create corporate cultures that encourage individual excellence for employees in their areas of specialty. Those employers able to do this first will have a better chance of holding on to their young managers and developing team players and leaders.

Up AND RUNNING

For consultants in the next century, it will be difficult to run any faster. Instead, they will have to spend a great deal more

179

time on self-education. But this, too, may be coming in the form of the personal computer. Think about the sophistication of some of the flight simulator programs developed in the past few years: Orbiter, Falcon-2, Fokker Tri-Plane, and so forth. Each is so complex and realistic that it requires almost a million bytes of memory to run. If such sophistication is transformed into development and training programs and general management education "expert systems," it may be possible for consultants and managers alike to educate themselves by accessing AI data banks at home or in their offices rather than in the classroom. In turn, such education could range from graduate-level studies of organization and compensation models in specific industries to complex engineering problems to help consulting engineers keep up to date, all of which could become the key process for national accreditation standards in our profession.

The accounting profession is showing us the lead today. To maintain one's accreditation, a CPA must study a certain number of hours and attend certain certified courses each month. Within the next decade, consultants should have to do the same. With so much time devoted to business development and self-development, there will be fewer hours available to deliver services, which, in turn, implies higher fees for the fewer available hours.

WHO GETS THE DECEASED'S ROYALTIES?

Not long ago at a meeting of the Dutch Institute of Management Consultants, I mused: With Artificial Intelligence coming along as it is, what will happen when all the consulting knowledge of all the great minds of McKinsey or Arthur Andersen is recorded and made available to clients? What happens when one of these major sources passes away? Who gets the royalties for the ideas provided through the medium of expert systems for the ensuing decades: the partnership, the widow, or the deceased's grandchildren? In our business, much of what we do is common sense, something that is useful for generations. The insights and strategies of a Peter Drucker, a Harry Levinson, a Kenichi Ohmae, a Michael Porter, and of many others will last far beyond their lives and probably will be applicable into the twenty-second century.

IMPLICATIONS OF PUBLIC OWNERSHIP

Before closing, I must note that there are some very disconcert-
ing issues facing the consulting industry. They are not new, but they are getting more visible. In 1970, the then head of ACME, Phil Shay, worried about the need of the largest consulting firms for ever-larger amounts of capital to maintain rapid growth and fund research. It was a phenomenon that Shay felt put dangerous pressures on the partners of these large firms to go public. Phil cautioned the industry that consulting firms that went public could end up so pressured to satisfy shareholders with current earnings and dividends that the quality of their services might be undermined through excessive cost-cutting and irrational productivity improvement campaigns.

Although little of this has come to pass, the opportunities for it to occur are greater than ever. Earlier I mentioned that Hay & Associates has been positively affected by the new Saatchi & Saatchi business development policies. The other side of the coin is that should such programs be taken to extremes, then the rewards within the firm will go to those most gifted with sales ability, not consulting skills, and promotion may become a sales contest far removed from the creation of permanent, positive change within client organizations. In fact, our clients are already becoming secondary to raw sales numbers. This theme is the battle flag taken up by McKinsey & Company and others who say they will never become publicly owned organizations.

Management consulting is a business where all of the most valuable assets walk home at night.

Those top minds, the best thinkers and consultants in any firm, are perfectly able to keep on walking should the conditions of their employment become odious. Organizations contemplating acquisitions in the management consulting field must take this into consideration when attempting a buy out.

182   But I am still optimistic. The marketplace has already rejected obsolete consultants and consulting firms in the past five years or so, and I believe the marketplace will also reject too slick and superficial an effort by any publicly held consulting firm in future. The practices that maintain professionalism will survive and thrive. That, in turn, requires a dedication to *quality staff* through selection and ongoing development, *quality services* through research and links with academia and *real value* delivered for the fees charged.

I have visions of some of the larger consulting firms expanding their marketing and delivery capabilities through the use of electronic networks by providing for a number of independents to "plug in" to their systems and provide subcontract assignments in markets where those firms are not represented at all. One of the areas where the Big-8 have a giant edge over some of the pure consulting firms is their network of offices. McKinsey, Booz, Allen, MAC, and others have no facilities in Louisville, Canton, Macon, Wilmington, Sacramento, Tallahassee, Austin, and dozens of other midsized cities. By having electronic "correspondents" in these locations, leading firms can expand their practices on a very cost-effective basis while controlling the quality of the work through nightly reviews, Socratic discussions via electronic messaging, and some of the advanced training programs described above.

If that kind of linkage is going to grow rapidly, then I believe the international linkage of the large and medium-sized firms will explode in the next decade. For a consulting firm to consider itself able to support a *Fortune* 1,000 client in the 1990s, it will have to have international capabilities. These are most likely to come through joint ventures and partnerships with overseas firms because that is the fastest and least costly method of international expansion. It is the principal reason for Temple, Barker and Sloane's sale to Marsh & McLennan and the ensuing access to their worldwide contacts. Almost immediately, TBS opened an office in London to begin penetrating the European market. Further, with European or Asian partners representing clients in those markets, client firms have natives able to help them in a broad range of marketing and strategy issues—something a purely United States-based partnership can't do in any event. The key to the best and most successful of these joint ventures and partnerships will rest with what the U.S. consulting firm has to offer its foreign consulting contacts and partners and their practices here in the United States.

CLIENT POWER

Perhaps the final apparent contradiction in terms has to do with the reality of client relations. Bob Atteyah, to cite him one last time, notes sagely that clients are still the ones who decide whether the work continues or not, based on their perception of the value they have or have not received. Clients, Atteyah points out, are very smart. They know who adds value, and they know who they want on a particular job. Selling stage two is totally dependent on doing stage one well. Even partnership is decided by the client, when you come right down to it!

In this profession, being right is easy. Effecting change is very hard. In the future consulting will entail organic approaches, preselling a wide range of executives, reaching an early consensus, if you will, about the problems and the issues, discussing how the client can use various solutions, and, finally, getting the client to take action. The absolutely worst consulting methodology today is the old mechanistic approach whereby the consultant visits the client, studies the issues, goes away, and writes a report. If the client is *really* interested in the report and wants to do something about it, the consultant is in trouble. When you use an organic approach, the client is implementing solutions while the report is still being drafted. The client becomes a part of the solution and gains a sense of ownership to assuring that changes will be implemented. Those consulting firms that are developing real expertise, innovation, and organic approaches to their clients, problems shouldn't have any trouble getting to the year 2001.

May you live in interesting times!

The Chinese meant it as a curse. The new consultants will find it a blessing.

RECOMMENDED READINGS

Babicky, J., "Consulting to the Family Business," *Journal of Management Consulting* 3 (4) (Fall 1987).

Bennington, L. A., and H. Swartz, "The CEO's Change Agenda," *Planning Review* 15 (3) (May-June 1987).

Buchholz, S., and T. Roth, *Creating the High-Performance Team: Wilson Learning Corporation* (New York: Wiley, 1987).

Davis, S. M., *Future Perfect* (Reading, Mass.: Addison-Wesley, 1987).

Drucker, P. F., "The Coming of the New Organization," *Harvard Business Review* (Jan.-Feb. 1988).

"A Sampling of Schools: The Boston Computer Society," *Computer Update* (Nov.-Dec. 1987).

INDEX

A

Academics, as independent
consultants, 35–37
Academy of Management, Management
Consultancy Division, 39, 40
Air California, 18
Alexander Proudfood, acquisition of,
33
American Can Co., rebirth and renewal
strategies, 91
American Express Co., response to
deregulation, 20
American Institute of Certified Public
Accountants (AICPA), 34
American Society of Training and
Development (ASTD), 46
American Telephone and Telegraph
(AT&T), as victim of deregulation,
19
as partners with Olivetti, 139
Apple Computer, technological
development, 174
Apregan, Craig, mismanagement
models, 175, 176
Argyris, Chris, on defensive routines,
8–9
Arthur Andersen & Co., as the largest
consulting organization, 25
market specialization, 30
technology training, 155–157
training investments, 58
Arthur D. Little, attempted takeover,
33
Arthur Young, size in the industry, 25
Artificial Intelligence (AI), 157–159
as a medium to expert knowledge,
181
as a source for consultant training,
180
Association of Consulting Management
Engineers (ACME), 39
A. T. Kearney, growth of firm, 26
logistics software, 26
Atteyah, Robert, on culture change,
85, 163
on client values, 183, 184

B

BancOne, Ohio, services marketing,
131
Bank of America, layoffs, 28
Big-8 accounting firms, organization
problems, 66–68
role in the industry, 26–28
Boston Consulting Group (BCG),
strategic planning models, 75
Bristol-Meyers, corporate culture, 51
British consulting firms, expansion into
the U.S., 32
British Management Consultancy
Associates, 31
Booz, Allen & Co., government
contracts, 26

C

Cambridge Energy Research Associates
(CERA), 27
Casio, global product strategy, 82
C.A.S.T. Management Consultants,
international expansion, 31
Champions, as leaders, 5–7
Chrysler Corp., competition with
General Motors, 10
international subsidiaries, 136
Clarke, Christopher, corporate life
cycles, 5–7, 125
Cleveland Consulting Associates,
acquisition of, 31
Clients,
dealing with change, 79–81
education consulting for, 157
international alliances, 136–138
managing change, 85–87
new demands of, 45–47
organization problems, 96–98
reward systems for, 113–127
"shadowing," 46
strategic services for, 75–93
Compensation,
global standards for, 15, 113–126
Competency testing for clients, 125
Computer Aided Design (CAD), 149

Computer Aided Manufacturing (CAM),
149, 150
Computer Numerical Control (CNC),
149
Content consulting style vs. process,
49–54
Consultants,
as expert witnesses, 54
to family-owned business services,
167–169
as public speakers, 62
publishing articles, 63, 64
qualifications, 48
to small business services, 164–167
staying effective, 172, 173
Consulting industry,
consolidation, 33, 34
international growth, 31–33
lack of leadership, 34
Coopers & Lybrand, 25
Cost Management, as a driving force,
16–17
Cresap, McCormick & Paget,
acquisition of, 33
Crisis consulting, 176–178
Cummings, Thomas G., on self-design,
52, 104, 152

D
Davis, John, on consulting to family
owned businesses, 168–171
De Benedetti, Count Carlo, 138–140
Deming, W. Edward, 50
Deregulation, continuing problems, 5
of banking, 19
of communications, 19
of transportation, 18
Drucker, Peter, on future organization
structures, 175

E
ECOTEC, international growth, 32
Egon Zender & Associates,
international expansion, 31
Electronic Data Services (EDS),
as AA competitor, 155
as a GM acquisition, 10
Ernst & Whinney, practice evolution,
68
Experience Curve Model, 9
Exports from the U. S., 4–5, 14–15,
132–135

F
Federal Express Corp., pay policies,
115
Ford Motor Co., corporate culture, 51
competition with General Motors, 10
international subsidiaries, 136

G
Gain sharing, 116, 119
Geneen, Harold T., 17
General Motors Corp.,
competition with Ford and Chrysler,
10
NUMI joint venture, 136
Genetic Imprinting of management
values, 9, 150
Gersick, Kelin, on consulting to family
owned businesses, 171, 172
Glassman, Alan,
on changing cultures, 51
on managerial self-denial, 7
on project management, 36
Global Markets, 13
Government, consulting to, 52, 53
Greenmail tactics, 18
Greiner, Larry E., on organizational
evolution, 97, 98, 109
Gulf & Western Industries, 91

H
Hall, William, on declining industries,
8
Handley-Walker Company,
international growth, 32
Harvard Business School,
distinctive competence concepts, 75
generalist consulting concepts, 47
Harvard M.B.A.s, cost of, 47
Hay & Associates, acquisition of, 31
business development, 66
recruitment away from, 96, 97
Henderson, Bruce, on strategic
services for clients, 92
Housekeepers, exercising control, 76
as leaders, 6–9
as lovers of quick fixes, 145
Hughes Aircraft, as a GM acquisition,
10

I
IBM, introducing technology, 153
competition with AA, 155

Inbucon, international mergers, 33
International Council of Management
    Consulting Institutes (ICMCI), 33
International partnerships to support
    client global competition, 135–
    140
International trade with Japan, 142
International Universal Consortium,
    consultant education, 58
Institute of Management Consultants
    (IMC), 38
Inventory Management, Just-In-Case
    vs. Just-In-Time, 16

J
Jobs, Steven, as organizational
    Champion, 5
John Deere Company, introduction of
    large-scale automation, 154

K
Kantor, Rosebeth Moss,
    compensation revolt, 115
Kaplan, Smith & Co., market
    specialization, 30
Kennedy, James M., *Directory of
    Management Consultants*, 27
Kepner-Tregoe, strategic services, 75
Kerr, Jeffrey, on reward systems and
    corporate culture, 118
Key Factors of Success, 17
Kibel, Green Corp., 26
Kienbaum & Associates, international
    expansion, 31
Kübler-Ross Model, psychological
    stages of man and organizations, 7

L
Lemon Squeezers, as leaders, 7
Levinson, Dr. Harry, on consulting
    challenges, 163, 164
Liker, Jeffrey, on automation
    implementation, 153

M
Machine Bureaucracies, compensation,
    113
    as organization model, 6, 7
Management Analysis Center (MAC),
    26
Management-by-Objectives (MBO), 21,
    22, 123

Management-by-Walking-Around
    (MBWA), 21
Managerial Self-Denial, 7–9
Marcory, Michael, on family attitudes
    and effects on work, 178, 179
Marketing, of consultant services, 61–
    72
Marketing services, for clients, 129–
    143
Mary Kay Cosmetics, as a model of
    sales management, 50
Mathews, Charles, crisis consulting
    analogies, 176–178
McKinsey & Co.,
    in Japan, 81
    on public ownership, 182
    size in the industry, 26, 27
Mechanistic Management, 10–12, 22,
    56–57, 71–72, 145–147
Mercer Meidinger, acquisition of, 33
Mintzberg, Henry, on Machine
    Bureaucracies, 6, 90
Mitroff, Ian, on contingency planning,
    77, 78
Morgan Stanley, white collar
    productivity, 156
Moses, as a biblical consultant to the
    Israelites, 163, 164

N
Nanus, Bert, future opportunities for
    consultants, 164
Naylor, Michael, exponential curve of
    change, 79, 90
Negotiation skills, 54
Networking, consultants use of for
    developing clients, 29

O
Ohmae, Kenichi, global strategies,
    81, 82
    technological development, 174
    Triad power, 135
Olivetti Corporation, as an
    international model for clients,
    138–140
Organic Management, 10–12, 56–57,
    71–72, 145–147
Organization *Birth*, 5
Organization *Decline*, 5
Organization design services, 95
Organization *Growth*, 5

Organization "Life Cycles," as per
    Clarke & Pratt, 5
Organization *Maturity*, 5–7
Organization *Rebirth & Renewal*, 29

P
P.A. Consulting Group Ltd.,
    international expansion, 31
Pacific Southwest Airlines (PSA), 18
Patton, General George S., as a Tank
    Commander, 6
Pay-for-performance plans, 116–118
Payne, Adrian, on strategic services of
    consulting firms, 90
Peat Marwick Main & Co.,
    advanced manufacturing systems,
    157
    practice evolution, 68
    size, 25
    strategic alliances, 35
Peat Marwick & McClintock, 32
P.E. International, international
    mergers, 33
Personal computers, use of by
    consultants, 69–71
Peters, Tom, on "Lemon Squeezers," 7
Pickens, T. Boone, "Greenmail"
    tactics, 18
Porter, Michael E., value-added
    pricing strategies, 37, 83–84
Pratt, Simon, corporate life cycles,
    5–8, 125
Process consulting, 49–54

Q
Quality Circles (QCs), their misuse, 21
    effective use of, 105
Quality Control (QC), 149
Quality Engineering (QE), 11

R
Reagan administration, levels of
    employment, 4
Reisman & Associates, executive
    selection and screening, 125
Robotics, 150–152

S
Saatchi & Saatchi, on acquisitions, 31
    performance results, 181

Sabath, Robert, on process
    consultants, 85
Schmenner, Roger, on management of
    service industries, 108, 109
Schonberger & Associates, 154
Self-design organization methods, 49,
    50, 100–108
Senn-Delaney & Associates, 30
Shay, Phillip, industry issues, 181,
    182
Slocum, John, on corporate culture and
    reward systems, 118
Spicer & Oppenheimer, market
    specialization, 30
Standards of performance for clients,
    119–112
Starr, Martin, on Japanese ownership of
    American firms, 147–149
Steinberg, Saul, "Greenmail" tactics,
    18
Steiner, George, 75
Strategic models, use of, 76, 78
    newest developments in, 91, 92
Strategic Planning Retreats, 88–90

T
Tank Commanders, as leaders, 5–7
Temple, Barker & Sloane, acquisition
    of, 33, 183
    international expansion, 26
Theodore Barry & Associates, 26
Time bankruptcy, impact on retail
    customers, 130
Toffler, Alvin, on second vs. third wave
    management, 4, 10
    on strategic planning, 77
Towers, Perrin, Forster & Crosby,
    acquisitions, 33, 35
    overseas expansion, 32
Tregoe, Benjamin, on strategic
    discipline. *See also* Kepner-
    Tregoe, 86
TRW Corporation, employee training
    expenditures, 151
Turnaround situations, consulting to,
    53, 54

U
University of Southern California,
    Center for Effective Organizations
    (CEO), 36, 104

190

Center for Crisis Management
    (CCM), 77
U. S. Congress, impact of deregulation,
    19–20
U. S. Export-Import Bank, as a
    consultant, 134
U. S. Government, consulting needs,
    31

V
Vector Analysis Marketing Model, 129

W,X,Y,Z
The Warner Group, 27
Wells Fargo Bank & Trust Co., on
    Crocker Merger, 28
Work design, as applied to clients,
    98, 99